The

3-Minute
BIBLE
HABIT

for Women

© 2022 by Barbour Publishing, Inc.

Print ISBN 978-1-63609-257-7

Published by Barbour Publishing, Inc., 1810 Barbour Drive, Uhrichsville, Ohio 44683, www.barbourbooks.com

Our mission is to inspire the world with the life-changing message of the Bible.

Printed in the United States of America.

Renée Sanford

The
3-Minute
BIBLE
HABIT
for Women

A 90-Day Plan for
Daily Quiet Time

BARBOUR
PUBLISHING

Before We Begin. . .

Congratulations! You're about to begin one of life's most rewarding habits. That habit is reading a set of Bible verses each day. The first set (Day 1) talks about enjoying the Bible's rich rewards. The second (Day 2) talks about the Bible's weight in gold. Take those two days to heart, and you'll be eager to keep reading!

Each day of this *3-Minute Bible Habit for Women* features three sections.

> Minute 1: Read God's Word ("The Bible Says" focuses on a few Bible verses followed by the references for each verse)

> Minute 2: Unpack God's Word through a devotional thought ("Consider")

> Minute 3: Apply God's Word to your life ("Ponder" three points)

It's completely optional, but sometimes you may want to read more about what the Bible says on a given topic. That's why additional Bible verse references appear in italics at the end of each day's reading.

One of the references at the end of Day 1 is Psalm 1:1–3. These three verses speak of the person who rejects worldly ways and who cherishes and embraces God's ways. Such a godly and righteous person enjoys God's blessings of peace and provision and success.

Happy is the man who does not walk in the way sinful men tell him to, or stand in the path of sinners, or sit with those who laugh at the truth. But he finds joy in the Law of the Lord and thinks about His Law day and night. This man is like a tree planted by rivers of water, which gives its fruit at the right time and its leaf never dries up. Whatever he does will work out well for him.

Do you want happiness and joy? Do you want peace and provision and success? If so, you have the right book in your hands!

This *3-Minute Bible Habit for Women* features Bible verses exclusively from the New Life Version. The next four pages, which are written by world-renowned missionary translators Gleason and Kathryn Ledyard, will help you appreciate this acclaimed, easy-to-read translation.

Introduction to the New Life Version

The idea of a very readable and yet accurate version of the scriptures came to us in an igloo in the frozen Canadian Arctic many years ago. A few of the First Nations people with whom we were working then were just starting to learn English. Although it was twenty years later before the New Life Version was published, the idea never left us.

Instead, during those years, vocabulary and thought patterns were observed, which helped set the course for the Bible translation featured in this book. This version has already been used and appreciated in many parts of the world where English is used as a second language.

The secret of its readability is in the limited vocabulary. In most cases, each word uses only one meaning. Difficult biblical words found in other versions were broken down into simple, meaningful phrases. Other problems in Bible reading were researched, and the end result is a very readable and understandable version. Even educated adults who are familiar with the scriptures find themselves startled into new insights by its blunt simplicity.

Those of us who worked on this limited-vocabulary New Life Version were constantly watching to keep it understandable without sacrificing accuracy. There was no thought to change God's holy Word to today's street language. In fact, in many places, the wording and beauty of older versions have been retained. Paraphrasing, or man's idea of what the Bible says, was ruled out. The careful and prayerful use of some basic words can be made to say what the original languages said, thus assuring the reader of an accurate text.

Two different times, the Bible speaks of the very words written by God and by Jesus Christ. Exodus 31:18 says, "When the Lord had finished speaking with Moses on Mount Sinai, He gave him the two stone writings of the Law, pieces of stone written on by the finger of God." And John 8:6 says, "Jesus got down and began to write in the dust with His finger." Both of these writings were soon destroyed. The pieces of stone with the written Law were broken in front of the children of Israel, who were worshipping a false god, and it was not long before the people walked over what Jesus had written on the ground. But it pleased God to have His law, and the good news of life that lasts forever, written by men He chose for that special job.

Those early men of God—who copied the words given by the Holy Spirit that make up the sixty-six books of the Bible—used different languages than are used today. From Genesis to Revelation forty different men were used over a period of 1,600 years. Four hundred years of time separated the Old Testament from the New. The way of life of the people living in Old Testament times was much different from those living during New Testament times. Hebrew was the language of the Old Testament, and Greek was used in the New Testament.

Those men did not write the Bible but were led or guided by the Holy Spirit as to what they wrote and the words to use. "Understand this first: No part of the Holy Writings was ever made up by any man. No part of the Holy Writings came long ago because of what man wanted to write. But holy men who belonged to God spoke what the Holy Spirit told them" (2 Peter 1:20–21).

The first copies of the holy scriptures were perfect and without error. But man is not perfect, and because of changes in languages through the many years and translation from one language to another, no version can claim that same degree of perfection.

Since about 1900, many different versions have been printed in English—and hundreds in other major languages and tribal languages around the world. In all these languages, God's written Word is alive today. Through the years, sinful men have tried to destroy it, but this living Book can never be destroyed. "Heaven and earth will pass away, but My words will not pass away" (Matthew 24:35).

The Word of God contains many promises. This one tells what reading the Bible will do: "All the Holy

Writings are God-given and are made alive by Him. Man is helped when he is taught God's Word. It shows what is wrong. It changes the way of a man's life. It shows him how to be right with God. It gives the man who belongs to God everything he needs to work well for Him" (2 Timothy 3:16–17).

We dedicate this New Life Version to Him in whose honor it has been published. May it give all who read it (1) a greater understanding of the scriptures and (2) a better knowledge of Jesus Christ, who came to save—from the penalty and power of sin—all who will put their trust in Him.

Gleason and Kathryn Ledyard

Day 1

Enjoy the Bible's Rich Rewards

THE BIBLE SAYS

Ezra had set his heart to learn the Law of the Lord, to live by it, and to teach His Laws.

How sweet is Your Word to my taste! It is sweeter than honey to my mouth!

Your words were found and I ate them. And Your words became a joy to me and the happiness of my heart. For I have been called by Your name, O Lord God of All.

[Jesus:] "If you know these things, you will be happy if you do them."

I pray that our faith together will help you know all the good things you have through Christ Jesus.

Bible References: Ezra 7:10, Psalm 119:103, Jeremiah 15:16, John 13:17, Philemon 6

CONSIDER

God promises many good gifts if we read His Word, think about it, and obey His commands. This theme echoes throughout scripture. We see it in the five Bible verses quoted above. We see it in the additional Bible verses listed below. You don't have to read all of them, of course. They're completely optional. After all, we promised this is *The 3-Minute Bible Habit for Women*, not the 6- or 9-Minute Bible Habit!

Throughout this book, we offer ninety of the Bible's many themes. Ultimately, we trust this book will make it easy for you to read, consider, and ponder God's Word three minutes daily. Enjoy!

PONDER

* Why would God repeat such extravagant promises over and over?

* Why does God want us to take Him at His Word at every turn?

* Is it really possible to enjoy God's good gifts in this life?

More about Enjoy the Bible's Rich Rewards: Joshua 1:7–9, Psalm 1:1–3, Psalm 19:7–14, Ezekiel 3:1–11, James 1:16–25

Day 2

The Bible's Weight in Gold

THE BIBLE SAYS

Gold. . .cannot be compared to it in worth and it cannot be traded for objects of fine gold.

The Word of the Lord is worth more than gold, even more than much fine gold.

The Law of Your mouth is better to me than thousands of gold and silver pieces.

I love Your Word more than gold, more than pure gold.

It is better than getting silver and fine gold.

Bible References: Job 28:17, Psalm 19:10, Psalm 119:72, Psalm 119:127, Proverbs 3:14

CONSIDER

Did you know five billion copies of the Bible are in print? What's more, the Bible has been published in 3,415 languages. No other book compares with the Bible—not even close! It's the greatest book ever written, published, and distributed worldwide.

The Bible is also called the Holy Bible, God's Word, and scripture. The first three-quarters of the Bible are called the Old Writings, that is, the Old Testament or the Hebrew scriptures. The final quarter of the Bible is called the New Writings, that is, the New Testament or the Christian scriptures.

The entire Bible is given by God to all humanity around the world and down through every age. What a great gift, indeed!

PONDER

* Imagine receiving a handwritten letter from God. What would you do with it?

* Imagine God giving you a bar of pure gold. Again, what would you do with it?

* Do you have your own Bible yet? If so, what do you want to do with it?

More about The Bible's Weight in Gold: Proverbs 8:10, Proverbs 8:19, Proverbs 16:16, Proverbs 20:15

Day 3

"The Lord God Said"

THE BIBLE SAYS

The Lord God said, "It is not good for man to be alone. I will make a helper that is right for him."

The Lord said to Abram, "Leave your country, your family and your father's house, and go to the land that I will show you."

After this, Moses and Aaron went to Pharaoh and said, "The Lord, the God of Israel, says this: 'Let My people go, that they may have a special supper to honor Me in the desert.'"

"Now, O Lord God, make sure forever the word which You have spoken about Your servant and his family. Do as You have said."

The Lord came to Solomon in a special dream in Gibeon during the night. God said, "Ask what you wish Me to give you."

Bible References: Genesis 2:18, Genesis 12:1, Exodus 5:1, 2 Samuel 7:25, 1 Kings 3:5

CONSIDER

In the Bible, God and the early preachers do most of the talking. Later, God told people what to write to be included in the greatest book in human history, the Bible. From cover to cover, the Bible declares what the Lord God said to Himself, to Adam and Eve, to Moses, to David, to Solomon, and to Isaiah, Jeremiah, Ezekiel, and other early preachers. It also declares what Jesus and His followers said in the New Writings. Let's listen!

PONDER

* What does "the Lord said" signify each time it appears in the Bible?

* Why do you think God often includes commands with promises?

* How would you probably feel if God spoke directly to you?

More about "The Lord God Said": Isaiah 28:16, Jeremiah 7:20, Ezekiel 2:4, Zechariah 11:4, Revelation 1:8

Day 4

God Divinely Inspired the Bible

THE BIBLE SAYS

[Jesus:] "I tell you, as long as heaven and earth last, not one small mark or part of a word will pass away of the Law of Moses until it has all been done."

"Abraham said, 'They have the Writings of Moses and of the early preachers. Let them hear what they say.' "

Jesus kept on telling them what Moses and all the early preachers had said about Him in the Holy Writings.

[Jesus:] "If you had believed Moses, you would believe Me. For Moses wrote about Me."

We always thank God that when you heard the Word of God from us, you believed it.

Bible References: Matthew 5:18, Luke 16:29, Luke 24:27, John 5:46, 1 Thessalonians 2:13

CONSIDER

Here are five of the many compelling reasons for God's inspiration of the Bible. First, the Bible is consistently called "the Word of God." Second, the Bible states directly that it is inspired by God. Third, the old preachers recognized God as their source. Fourth, Jesus Christ fully supported all of scripture. Fifth, the followers of Jesus viewed both the Old Writings and their inspired writings as the Word of God, holy scripture.

PONDER

* Is it easy or hard for you to believe God inspired the Bible?

* What makes it easiest for you to believe this truth?

* What makes it hardest for you to believe this truth?

More about God Divinely Inspired the Bible: Jeremiah 36:27, Luke 24:44, Titus 1:3, Hebrews 1:1, Hebrews 4:12, 2 Peter 3:2

Still more: Deuteronomy 18:15–22, Acts 7:38, 1 Corinthians 10:1–11, 1 Timothy 4:1–3, 1 Peter 1:23–25, 2 Peter 3:15–16, Revelation 1:1–3

Day 5

Jeremiah on God's Inspiration of Scripture

THE BIBLE SAYS

"Read to the people the words of the Lord which you have written down as I told them to you."

They asked Baruch, "Tell us, how did you write all this? Did Jeremiah tell it to you?"

Elnathan and Delaiah and Gemariah begged the king not to burn the book, but he would not listen to them.

"Take another book and write in it all the words that were in the first book which Jehoiakim the king of Judah burned."

Then Jeremiah took another book and gave it to Baruch the son of Neraiah, the writer. And as Jeremiah told them to him, he wrote down all the words of the book which Jehoiakim king of Judah had burned in the fire. And many words of the same kind were added to them.

Bible References: Jeremiah 36:6, Jeremiah 36:17, Jeremiah 36:25, Jeremiah 36:28, Jeremiah 36:32

CONSIDER

No prophet tells us more about God's inspiration of the Bible than Jeremiah. First, inspiration often begins as an oral message that the old preacher dictates or pens. Second, inspiration is exclusively God's message to humanity through human instruments and their secretaries. Third, inspiration is always dependent on the Lord. Fourth, inspiration applies to the very choice of words. Yes, Jeremiah also wrote down his own thoughts and the remarks of others, but the Holy Spirit directed every word he wrote.

PONDER

* If God hadn't inspired him, how much do you think Jeremiah would have written?

* Why did Jeremiah keep writing after his first copy was destroyed by the king?

* What would be the highs and lows of being inspired to write God's Word, as Jeremiah was?

More about Jeremiah on God's Inspiration of Scripture: Jeremiah 36:1–4, Jeremiah 36:9–16, Jeremiah 36:22–23, Jeremiah 42:4, Jeremiah 42:7, Jeremiah 43:1

Day 6

The Holy Spirit Inspired Scripture

THE BIBLE SAYS

"The Spirit of the Lord spoke by me. His Word was on my tongue."

"You spoke sharp words to them by Your Spirit through the men who tell what will happen."

When He spoke to me, the Spirit came into me and set me on my feet. I heard Him speaking to me.

"They could not hear the Law and the words which the Lord of All had sent by His Spirit through the men who spoke for Him in the past."

No part of the Holy Writings came long ago because of what man wanted to write. But holy men who belonged to God spoke what the Holy Spirit told them.

Bible References: 2 Samuel 23:2, Nehemiah 9:30, Ezekiel 2:2, Zechariah 7:12, 2 Peter 1:21

CONSIDER

Throughout the Bible, the early preachers affirmed the

Holy Spirit's inspiration of their writings. This is true of David, Nehemiah, Ezekiel, Zechariah, and other prophets. This also is true of Jesus Christ's followers including Matthew, Mark, Luke, John, Peter, Paul, James, and Jude. The latter two were half brothers of Jesus. They all knew Him very well. Still, they relied on the Holy Spirit to inspire every word they wrote.

PONDER

* Did you know David wrote many things mentioned but not included in scripture?

* Did you know Solomon wrote extensively beyond what's included in the Bible?

* How do you think they knew when the Holy Spirit was inspiring their words?

More about The Holy Spirit Inspired Scripture: Matthew 22:43, Mark 12:36, Acts 1:16, Acts 4:25, Ephesians 6:17, 2 Timothy 4:1, Hebrews 1:1

Day 7

What We Can Know "For Sure"

THE BIBLE SAYS

[Jesus] said, "For sure, I tell you, unless you have a change of heart and become like a little child, you will not get into the holy nation of heaven."

[Jesus:] "For sure, I tell you, whoever does not receive the holy nation of God as a child will not go into the holy nation."

Jesus said to [Nicodemus], "For sure, I tell you, unless a man is born again, he cannot see the holy nation of God."

[Jesus:] "For sure, I tell you, anyone who hears My Word and puts his trust in Him Who sent Me has life that lasts forever. He will not be guilty. He has already passed from death into life."

[Jesus:] "So if the Son makes you free, you will be free for sure."

Bible References: Matthew 18:3, Luke 18:17, John 3:3, John 5:24, John 8:36

CONSIDER

Jesus assured His followers of many important truths. In particular, He used the phrase "For sure" to emphasize some of those important truths. Those truths pertain to God and His Word. They also pertain to how to become a Christian. Becoming a Christian is a rebirth from your earthly family to God's forever family. Nothing is more exciting!

PONDER

* ✳ Truth isn't all relative. We can know "for sure."

* ✳ If the Lord God said it, we can know it "for sure."

* ✳ If Jesus said it, we can know it "for sure" as well.

More about What We Can Know "For Sure": Matthew 13:17, Mark 9:41, Mark 10:15, Mark 12:43, Luke 17:1, Luke 18:29–30, Luke 23:43, John 6:47, John 8:31, John 8:34

Day 8

God's Predictions Always Come True (1 of 2)

THE BIBLE SAYS

So Moses the servant of the Lord died there in the land of Moab, as the Word of the Lord said.

"The Lord has done what He said He would do."

The king did not listen to the people. The Lord had let this happen, that He might keep His Word, which the Lord spoke through Ahijah the Shilonite to Jeroboam the son of Nebat.

"It was done as had been spoken to him by the word of the Lord."

This was done so the word of the Lord spoken by Jeremiah came true.

Bible References: Deuteronomy 34:5, 1 Samuel 28:17, 1 Kings 12:15, 1 Kings 13:26, 2 Chronicles 36:21

CONSIDER

God knew everything before He spoke the word to

create the heavens and earth. So, it shouldn't surprise us that God can predict and prophesy what will happen. In the Bible, He predicts what will happen in the near future, in the distant future, at the climax of history, and beyond.

PONDER

* If God always has known everything, is He ever shocked or surprised?

* If God knows everything, why are people so reluctant to believe Him?

* God doesn't give His predictions in consecutive order all at once. Just the opposite. When a given prediction doesn't seem to make sense by itself, what can we do?

More about God's Predictions Always Come True: Exodus 8:20–24, Deuteronomy 18:18–32, 2 Kings 23:26–27, 2 Chronicles 10:15, Nehemiah 9:32

Still more: Isaiah 46:10, Jeremiah 32:8, Jeremiah 40:2–3, Lamentations 2:17, Daniel 4:33, Daniel 9:4, Joel 2:28–32, Amos 3:7, Zechariah 1:6, Acts 2:16–21

Day 9

God's Predictions Always Come True (2 of 2)

THE BIBLE SAYS

This happened as the Lord said it would happen through the early preacher.

[Jesus:] "This has happened as the early preachers said in the Holy Writings it would happen."

[Jesus:] "All things will happen as it is written."

[Jesus:] "All things written about Me in the Law of Moses and in the Books of the early preachers and in the Psalms must happen as they said they would happen."

"God did what He said He would do through all the early preachers."

Bible References: Matthew 1:22, Matthew 26:56, Luke 21:22, Luke 24:44, Acts 3:18

CONSIDER

As we saw yesterday, God always did (and will continue

to do) what He predicted through His old preachers. This includes all the Old Testament prophets. This also includes what Jesus said to His apostles in the Gospels, the Letters, and the book of Revelation. These predictions often had to do with Jesus Christ coming not just once (as a baby in Bethlehem) but a second time (to judge the world). God made all the predictions come true about Christ's first coming.

PONDER

* Do you have any favorite predictions that "came true" when Jesus was born?

* Jesus Himself repeatedly told His disciples that He would die and come back to life (Good Friday and Easter). How well did His followers understand what He said?

* Do you find it easy or hard to believe in Jesus Christ's second coming?

More about God's Predictions Always Come True: Matthew 26:24, Mark 9:13, John 17:12, 2 Corinthians 1:20, 2 Peter 1:19–21, Revelation 10:7

Day 10

Delight in God's Word

THE BIBLE SAYS

Happy are those whose way is without blame, who walk in the Law of the Lord. Happy are those who keep His Law and look for Him with all their heart. They also do not sin, but walk in His ways.

Your Law is my joy and it tells me what to do.

Make me walk in the path of Your Word, for I find joy in it.

I will be glad in Your Law, which I love.

I have been given Your Law forever. It is the joy of my heart.

Bible References: Psalm 119:1–3, Psalm 119:24, Psalm 119:35, Psalm 119:47, Psalm 119:111

CONSIDER

With 176 verses, Psalm 119 is the longest chapter in the Bible. All the way through, the psalmist repeatedly affirms his delight in God's Word. To do so, he repeatedly uses ten different terms for the Old Writings.

What's more, the psalmist's delight in scripture continues no matter what happens, even when he faces difficult people and perilous situations. Because he delights in the Bible, he finds it easy to remember its most important truths to affirm, commands to obey, and examples to heed in daily living.

Like the psalmist, may we never let anything rob us of delighting in scripture. May it always be our delight!

PONDER

* What are three memories you have of experiencing pure delight?

* What is it about the Bible that produces the most delight for you?

* How can embracing specific Bible truths bring you much delight?

More about Delight in God's Word: Psalm 119:70, Psalm 119:77, Psalm 119:92, Psalm 119:143, Psalm 119:174

Day 11

Embrace What Is
True and Trustworthy

THE BIBLE SAYS

Every good promise which the Lord had made to the people of Israel came true.

"Not one of all the good promises the Lord your God made to you has been broken. All have come true."

"You have done what You promised, for You are right and good."

"Then You came down on Mount Sinai and spoke with them from heaven. You gave them Laws that are right and true and good."

Every word of God has been proven true. He is a safe-covering to those who trust in Him.

Bible References: Joshua 21:45, Joshua 23:14, Nehemiah 9:8, Nehemiah 9:13, Proverbs 30:5

CONSIDER

God is always true and trustworthy. It's who God is.

Therefore, God's Word is always true and trustworthy. It reflects the nature of the One who has spoken to us. If we're smart (and we are, aren't we?), we want to wholeheartedly believe what is true and live accordingly. Therefore, we will set highest priority on listening to God's inspired Word, the Bible.

PONDER

* ✳ "God cannot lie." Why or why not? What do you believe?

* ✳ Do you find it easy or hard to believe God's promises?

* ✳ Do you find it easy or hard to believe His miracles?

More about Embrace What Is True and Trustworthy: 1 Samuel 2:34, 2 Kings 15:12, Psalm 18:30, Psalm 19:9, Psalm 119:160

Still more: 2 Corinthians 3:14, Ephesians 1:13, Ephesians 4:14, Colossians 1:23, 1 Timothy 1:15, 1 Timothy 4:10, 2 Timothy 2:25, 1 John 5:10, Revelation 22:6

God Has Protected His Word

THE BIBLE SAYS

For the Word of the Lord is right. He is faithful in all He does.

Forever, O Lord, Your Word will never change in heaven.

The grass dries up. The flower loses its color. But the Word of our God stands forever.

[Jesus:] "I tell you, as long as heaven and earth last, not one small mark or part of a word will pass away of the Law of Moses until it has all been done."

You have been given a new birth. It was from a seed that cannot die. This new life is from the Word of God which lives forever. All people are like grass. Their greatness is like the flowers. The grass dries up and the flowers fall off. But the Word of the Lord will last forever. That Word is the Good News which was preached to you.

Bible References: Psalm 33:4, Psalm 119:89, Isaiah 40:8, Matthew 5:18, 1 Peter 1:23–25

CONSIDER

God is the great communicator, and He has a message for the world. He gave that message in the Bible, His scripture, written for all people to receive. Throughout history, and even today, wicked tyrants have tried to destroy the Bible, God's holy scripture. They always fail because nothing can defeat God or His purposes. His Word will not "go away," and it will never fail.

PONDER

* Why would wicked tyrants try to destroy all copies of the Bible?

* In such desperate times, what do God's people always do?

* If God treasures the Bible so much, what about you?

More about God Has Protected His Word: Deuteronomy 4:2, Psalm 19:7, Psalm 119:42, Psalm 119:111, Revelation 22:18–19

Day 13

Know God's Word (1 of 2)

THE BIBLE SAYS

I will be glad in Your Law. I will not forget Your Word.

Your Word is a lamp to my feet and a light to my path.

They said to each other, "Were not our hearts filled with joy when [Jesus] talked to us on the road about what the Holy Writings said?"

Then [Jesus] opened their minds to understand the Holy Writings.

[Jesus:] "The Holy Writings say that rivers of living water will flow from the heart of the one who puts his trust in Me." Jesus said this about the Holy Spirit Who would come to those who put their trust in Him.

Bible References: Psalm 119:16, Psalm 119:105, Luke 24:32, Luke 24:45, John 7:38–39

CONSIDER

We have ready access to the complete Bible in our own language. What a treasure! This book in your hands directly quotes 450 Bible verses. That's 1 out of every 69 verses in God's Word. What's more, you're learning about 90 key themes featured repeatedly in scripture. It's amazing what you can accomplish reading *The 3-Minute Bible Habit for Women*. Keep going strong!

PONDER

* The Holy Spirit brings God's Word alive within us. Ask Him to do just that today.

* Jesus knew the Holy Writings in great depth. Like Jesus, endeavor to do the same.

* God the Father gave us His Son, His Holy Spirit, and His Word. Receive all three.

More about Know God's Word: Matthew 22:29, Luke 24:27, Acts 18:28, Romans 1:2, Romans 12:1–2, 1 Corinthians 15:3–4

Day 14

Know God's Word (2 of 2)

THE BIBLE SAYS

After Jesus had been raised from the dead, His followers remembered He said this. They believed the Holy Writings and what He had said.

Philip started with this part of the Holy Writings and preached the Good News of Jesus to him.

Paul went in as he always did. They gathered together each Day of Rest for three weeks and he taught them from the Holy Writings.

Everything that was written in the Holy Writings long ago was written to teach us. By not giving up, God's Word gives us strength and hope.

Your heart should be holy and set apart for the Lord God. Always be ready to tell everyone who asks you why you believe as you do. Be gentle as you speak and show respect.

Bible References: John 2:22, Acts 8:35, Acts 17:2, Romans 15:4, 1 Peter 3:15

CONSIDER

After Jesus returned to heaven, God the Father gave Him authority to send the Holy Spirit to live inside all His followers. *All* doesn't refer to the first followers. Instead, *all* refers to all followers of Jesus Christ around the world and down through the ages. *All* have the Holy Spirit, who helps us understand the whole message of God.

PONDER

* ✳ Why do you think the Old Writings meant so much to Jesus and His followers?

* ✳ Why do you think Christians still include the Old Testament within their Bibles?

* ✳ Do you ask the Holy Spirit to help you understand God's Word? He is eager to do that!

More about Know God's Word: 1 Timothy 4:13, 2 Timothy 2:15, 2 Timothy 3:15–17, Hebrews 4:12, 2 Peter 1:20, 2 Peter 3:16

Day 15

God Keeps His Promises

THE BIBLE SAYS

"Know then that the Lord your God is God, the faithful God. He keeps His promise and shows His loving-kindness to those who love Him and keep His Laws, even to a thousand family groups in the future."

"By this the Lord is proving that He keeps the promise He made to your fathers, to Abraham, Isaac and Jacob."

"Thanks be to the Lord. . . . He has done all that He promised. Every word has come true of all His good promise."

We who have turned to Him can have great comfort knowing that He will do what He has promised.

The Lord is not slow about keeping His promise.

Bible References: Deuteronomy 7:9, Deuteronomy 9:5, 1 Kings 8:56, Hebrews 6:18, 2 Peter 3:9

CONSIDER

God always tells the truth, and He always keeps every

promise He has made. We want to be sure to claim God's promises meant for us today. Each of these promises applies to millions of Christians around the world. There is no such thing as a New Testament promise of God that applies only to your group or only to you.

PONDER

* What God says about Himself is always true.

* What Jesus promises His followers is always true as well.

* Ask the Holy Spirit to guide you as you look for God's promises today.

More about God Keeps His Promises: Deuteronomy 8:18, Joshua 14:10, 2 Samuel 22:31, 1 Kings 8:15, 1 Kings 8:24, Nehemiah 1:5, Psalm 119:41

Still more: Acts 2:38–39, Ephesians 3:6, Titus 1:2, Hebrews 4:1, Hebrews 10:23, Hebrews 12:26

Day 16

The Trinity:
Father, Son, and Holy Spirit

THE BIBLE SAYS

[Jesus:] "Go and make followers of all the nations. Baptize them in the name of the Father and of the Son and of the Holy Spirit."

The Holy Spirit came down on [Jesus] in a body like a dove. A voice came from heaven and said, "You are My much-loved Son. I am very happy with You."

[Jesus:] "The Helper is the Holy Spirit. The Father will send Him in My place."

You were made right with God through our Lord Jesus Christ by the Spirit of our God.

I pray that the great God and Father of our Lord Jesus Christ may give you the wisdom of His Spirit.

Bible References: Matthew 28:19, Luke 3:22, John 14:26, 1 Corinthians 6:11, Ephesians 1:17

CONSIDER

The Bible's greatest theme is who God is. The Bible

teaches the one true God is the Three-in-One God. That is, He is a Trinity: God the Father (often "God" and "Father" and "Father in heaven"), God the Son (often "Jesus" and "Christ"), and God the Holy Spirit (often "Spirit" and "God's Spirit").

PONDER

* Your heavenly Father loves you!

* Jesus Himself loves you!

* The Holy Spirit loves you!

More about The Trinity: Father, Son, and Holy Spirit: Genesis 1:1–2, Isaiah 48:16, Matthew 3:16–17, Luke 1:35, John 14:16–17, John 15:26, Acts 1:4, Acts 10:38

Still more: Romans 1:4, Romans 8:9, Romans 14:17–18, 1 Corinthians 12:4–6, 2 Corinthians 1:21–22, 2 Corinthians 13:14, Galatians 4:6, Ephesians 1:13–14, Ephesians 2:18, Ephesians 2:22, Ephesians 4:4–6, Titus 3:6, Hebrews 9:14, 1 Peter 1:2, Jude 20–21

Day 17

Is God Your Father?

THE BIBLE SAYS

"You did not think of the Rock Who gave you birth. You forgot the God Who gave you birth."

God in His holy house is a father to those who have no father. And He keeps the women safe whose husbands have died.

"He will cry to Me, 'You are my Father, my God, and the rock that saves me.' "

For You are our Father. Even though Abraham does not know us, and Israel does not see who we are, You, O Lord, are our Father.

But now, O Lord, You are our Father. We are the clay, and You are our pot maker.

Bible References: Deuteronomy 32:18, Psalm 68:5, Psalm 89:26, Isaiah 63:16, Isaiah 64:8

CONSIDER

The old preachers rarely spoke of God as Father. Over the past two thousand years, however, Christians have spoken of God as their heavenly Father, of Jesus Christ as God the Son (true God, true man), and of themselves as children of God (see "Still more" below).

PONDER

* How is God your heavenly Father?

* How is Jesus uniquely God the Son?

* Who are the children of God?

More about Is God Your Father?: John 3:35, John 5:17–23, John 6:37–39, John 10:15–18, John 10:29–30, John 13:1–3, John 14:6–13, John 14:20–31, John 15:8–10, John 16:25–27, John 17:1–5, John 20:21, Acts 2:33

Still more: Romans 8:15, Galatians 4:6, Ephesians 1:17, Ephesians 6:23, Philippians 2:11, Colossians 1:19, Colossians 3:17, 1 Thessalonians 3:13, 2 Thessalonians 2:16, Hebrews 1:3–5, Hebrews 12:9, James 1:27, 1 Peter 1:17, 2 Peter 1:17, 1 John 2:1, 1 John 3:1, Revelation 1:6

Day 18

Power of the Holy Spirit (1 of 2)

THE BIBLE SAYS

The Spirit of the Lord came upon Samson with power.

Then the Spirit of the Lord came upon him with power.

"Then the Spirit of the Lord will come upon you with power. You will speak God's Word with them and be changed into another man."

The Spirit of God came upon him with power, so that he spoke God's Word with them.

Then Samuel took the horn of oil and poured the oil on him in front of his brothers. The Spirit of the Lord came upon David with strength from that day on.

Bible References: Judges 14:6, Judges 14:19, 1 Samuel 10:6, 1 Samuel 10:10, 1 Samuel 16:13

CONSIDER

Three dramatic examples of the Holy Spirit coming with power on someone include mighty judge Samson, halfhearted King Saul, and wholehearted King David. A number of other examples from the Old Writings could be given (see "More about" below). Back then, the Holy Spirit came with power on specific individuals and occasionally on specific groups, but only temporarily.

Everything changed when Jesus came, rose from the dead, and returned to heaven. A few days later, Jesus sent the Holy Spirit to empower every Christian then and now.

Ask God to empower you by His Spirit today!

PONDER

* Samson should have honored God with his feats of strength.

* Saul should have humbled himself when the Holy Spirit left him.

* David grieved the Spirit whenever he disobeyed God's Word.

More about Power of the Holy Spirit: Numbers 11:17, Numbers 11:25, Judges 15:14, 1 Samuel 11:6, 1 Samuel 16:13, Micah 3:8, Zechariah 4:6

Day 19

Power of the Holy Spirit (2 of 2)

THE BIBLE SAYS

Jesus went back to Galilee in the power of the Holy Spirit.

[Jesus:] "But you will receive power when the Holy Spirit comes into your life. You will tell about Me. . . to the ends of the earth."

What I had to say when I preached was not in big sounding words of man's wisdom. But it was given in the power of the Holy Spirit.

I pray that because of the riches of His shining-greatness, He will make you strong with power in your hearts through the Holy Spirit.

The Good News did not come to you by word only, but with power and through the Holy Spirit.

Bible References: Luke 4:14, Acts 1:8, 1 Corinthians 2:4, Ephesians 3:16, 1 Thessalonians 1:5

CONSIDER

Can you name a few of your all-time favorite—wow!—miracles of Jesus? The Holy Spirit empowered Jesus to do hundreds of such miracles and to teach others for hundreds of hours throughout Galilee, Samaria, Judea, and at least three foreign excursions.

After His ascension back to heaven, Jesus sent the Holy Spirit to live in and empower every Christian. The Holy Spirit doesn't come and go. Instead, He flows best in and through us when we're fully committed to following the Lord.

PONDER

* Imagine what the Holy Spirit can do in and through you.

* Are you fully committed to following the Lord Jesus?

* If so, ask the Holy Spirit to empower you today!

More about Power of the Holy Spirit: Matthew 3:11, Luke 1:17, Luke 1:35, Luke 3:16, Acts 10:38, Romans 1:4, Romans 15:19, Galatians 4:29, Ephesians 6:18

Day 20

God Answers Prayer

THE BIBLE SAYS

Those who are right with the Lord cry, and He hears them. And He takes them from all their troubles.

For the Lord hears those who are in need.

Do not worry. Learn to pray about everything. Give thanks to God as you ask Him for what you need.

Let us go with complete trust to the throne of God. We will receive His loving-kindness and have His loving-favor to help us whenever we need it.

The prayer from the heart of a man right with God has much power.

Bible References: Psalm 34:17, Psalm 69:33, Philippians 4:6, Hebrews 4:16, James 5:16

CONSIDER

Imagine Jesus sitting at the right hand of the Father in heaven praying very specifically for you right now. He knows just what we need. Will the Father gladly say yes? Of course!

Imagine the Holy Spirit in your heart praying earnestly for you with heartfelt sounds way beyond words. He always asks according to God's will, and the Father knows exactly what the Spirit is asking. Again, He gladly says yes.

Imagine your own prayers to the Father. He will always answer. True, we often don't know what is best, so God may say no or not now. Then again, when the Father says yes, it is always better than what we could ask for! So, pray!

PONDER

* Like the psalmist, pray about your deepest hurts and needs.

* Can you visualize how glad God is to hear you?

* Can you trust God to answer yes in a way that is best for you?

More about God Answers Prayer: Psalm 116:1, Psalm 145:18, Proverbs 15:29, Matthew 7:7, John 14:13–14, John 15:7, 1 John 5:14–15

Day 21

God Is Always Right, Good, and Fair

THE BIBLE SAYS

"I will make known the name of the Lord. I will tell of the greatness of God! The Rock! His work is perfect. All His ways are right and fair. A God Who is faithful and without sin, right and good is He."

"O Lord God of Israel, You are right and good."

I will give thanks to the Lord because He is right and good. I will sing praise to the name of the Lord Most High.

But the Lord of All will be honored in what is right and fair. The holy God will show Himself holy in what is right and good.

"I am the Lord who shows loving-kindness and does what is fair and right and good on earth. For I find joy in these things," says the Lord.

Bible References: Deuteronomy 32:3–4, Ezra 9:15, Psalm 7:17, Isaiah 5:16, Jeremiah 9:24

CONSIDER

God is always right, good, and fair in all He says and does. The Old Writings make a big deal about this. The old preachers talked often about sin (and how much God hates it) because sin is all that is opposite of the truth, goodness, and love of God.

PONDER

* When God says He is "good," that means always. We never have to worry about catching Him on a "bad day."

* Do you secretly fear God will be less than good and loving to you?

* Think about yourself on your best day. Even then, are you better and more loving than God?

More about God Is Always Right, Good, and Fair: Psalm 9:16, Psalm 11:7, Psalm 45:6, Psalm 101:1, Psalm 103:6, Isaiah 1:27, Isaiah 61:8, Jeremiah 11:20

Day 22

God Knows Everything

THE BIBLE SAYS

"The secret things belong to the Lord our God. But the things that are made known belong to us and to our children forever, so we may obey all the words of this Law."

"You alone know the hearts of all the children of men."

Great is our Lord, and great in power. His understanding has no end.

"You are great in wisdom and powerful in Your works. Your eyes are open to all the ways of men."

Daniel said, "Let the name of God be honored forever and ever, for wisdom and power belong to Him."

Bible References: Deuteronomy 29:29, 1 Kings 8:39, Psalm 147:5, Jeremiah 32:19, Daniel 2:20

CONSIDER

God is far wiser than anyone can imagine. What's more, God is the source of all true knowledge and wisdom.

Sure, God knows all the facts in the universe, but God knows much, much more.

Remember phone books? A million facts but none that could change your life. By themselves, facts are stupid. God not only has all knowledge but also all discernment, all insight, all understanding, all wisdom, and way-above-our-heads ways.

PONDER

* None of us knows 0.000001 percent of what's true, right, important, and life-changing.

* So why in the world are we ever tempted to think we know better than God?

* Humbly acknowledge God's higher, heavenly wisdom and ways today.

More about God Knows Everything: Genesis 20:6, 1 Kings 4:29, 1 Chronicles 29:17, Psalm 44:21, Psalm 94:11, Proverbs 2:6, Proverbs 24:12

Still more: Matthew 6:4, Luke 16:15, Acts 15:8, Romans 11:33, Romans 16:27, 1 Corinthians 1:20–25, Colossians 2:3, James 1:5

God Is King Over All

THE BIBLE SAYS

"Let the heavens be glad. Let the earth be filled with joy. And let them say among the nations, 'The Lord rules!' "

The Lord is King forever and ever.

The Lord sits as King forever.

God rules over the nations. God sits on His holy throne.

"Thanks to our God. For the Lord our God is King. He is the All-powerful One."

Bible References: 1 Chronicles 16:31, Psalm 10:16, Psalm 29:10, Psalm 47:8, Revelation 19:6

CONSIDER

Our modern ideas about royalty are more romantic than awe-inspiring. But the Lord God's "Kingship" means He has the authority and right to govern the whole world and to govern our individual lives. What gives God this right to rule all of us and each of us?

He spoke everything into existence, and no power or creature in the spiritual world is anywhere close to being His equal. He, and He alone, is the Lord and King over all!

PONDER

* Who is the most famous or powerful person you have ever met?

* After you met them, did they get to know you let alone help you in tangible ways?

* Are you willing and ready to say, "The Lord God, the All-powerful, is my one and only King of kings"?

More about God Is King Over All: 1 Chronicles 29:11, Psalm 2:4, Psalm 9:7, Psalm 11:4, Psalm 22:28, Psalm 93:1, Psalm 97:1, Psalm 99:1, Psalm 103:19, Psalm 146:10, Isaiah 52:7, Daniel 5:21, Acts 4:24, Romans 9:5, 1 Timothy 6:15–16, Revelation 1:6

Day 24

God's Shining-Greatness

THE BIBLE SAYS

"But for sure, as I live, all the earth will be filled with the shining-greatness of the Lord."

"O Lord, You have great power, shining-greatness and strength. Yes, everything in heaven and on earth belongs to You. You are the King, O Lord. And You are honored as head over all."

O Lord, our Lord, how great is Your name in all the earth. You have set Your shining-greatness above the heavens.

The Lord is high above all nations. His shining-greatness is above the heavens.

One called out to another and said, "Holy, holy, holy, is the Lord of All. The whole earth is full of His shining-greatness."

Bible References: Numbers 14:21, 1 Chronicles 29:11, Psalm 8:1, Psalm 113:4, Isaiah 6:3

CONSIDER

The earth is filled with the Lord's shining-greatness. What's more, all shining-greatness belongs to the Lord forever and ever. Another word for *shining-greatness* is *glory*. Here on earth, we feel excitement when someone relatively rich or famous walks into the room. A certain buzz sweeps across the room. If they throw a brief smile in our direction, all the better. Now, imagine suddenly appearing before God's throne in heaven. *That* is the Lord's shining-greatness penetrating every subatomic particle in your body. Glory, indeed!

PONDER

* Remember a time when you experienced shining-greatness in the beauty of nature.

* Have you ever experienced that in a relationship—with your family or friends?

* Imagine what it would be like to experience that with God—because someday you will!

More about God's Shining-Greatness: Psalm 29:1, Psalm 148:13, Isaiah 42:8, Jude 25, Revelation 4:11, Revelation 5:12–13

Day 25

With God All Things Are Possible

THE BIBLE SAYS

"Is anything too hard for the Lord?"

The Lord made it possible for her to have a child and she gave birth to a son.

"I know that You can do all things. Nothing can put a stop to Your plans."

Jesus looked at them and said, "This cannot be done by men. But with God all things can be done."

"God can do all things."

Bible References: Genesis 18:14, Ruth 4:13, Job 42:2, Matthew 19:26, Luke 1:37

CONSIDER

Humanly speaking, God's powerful works are *impossible*. Of course, God just smiles! When it comes to God's powerful works, three facts resound throughout the Bible. First, God made the heavens and earth from nothing. Second, God can do whatever He wants.

Third, God has done—and will do—astounding works that shatter humanity's faulty perceptions of full knowledge, full predictability, and full control. Whatever God does is astounding.

PONDER

* When your life starts to feel completely out of control, what's your first response?

* When you are facing the biggest challenge of your life, what's your best response?

* When your future seems bleak, clouded, and dark, what's your smartest response?

More about With God All Things Are Possible: Deuteronomy 10:21, Judges 13:3, 1 Samuel 1:20, 1 Samuel 12:24, 2 Samuel 7:21, Job 5:9, Job 9:10, Job 37:5, Psalm 9:1, Psalm 71:19, Psalm 72:18, Psalm 73:28, Psalm 75:1, Psalm 77:12, Psalm 78:4, Psalm 86:10, Psalm 98:1, Psalm 126:3, Isaiah 12:5, Isaiah 25:1, Isaiah 45:7, Isaiah 46:10, Jeremiah 33:3, Zechariah 8:6

Still more: Mark 14:36, Luke 1:49, Luke 9:43, Luke 13:17, Luke 18:27, Ephesians 1:19-20, Hebrews 5:9, 2 Peter 1:3-4, Jude 25, Revelation 15:3

Day 26

The Lord God Created All Things

THE BIBLE SAYS

This is the story of the heavens and the earth when they were made, in the day the Lord God made the earth and the heavens.

"For in six days the Lord made the heavens, the earth, the sea and all that is in them."

The heavens were made by the Word of the Lord. All the stars were made by the breath of His mouth.

"O Lord God! See, You have made the heavens and the earth by Your great power and by Your long arm! Nothing is too hard for You!"

Christ made everything in the heavens and on the earth. He made everything that is seen and things that are not seen. He made all the powers of heaven. Everything was made by Him and for Him.

Bible References: Genesis 2:4, Exodus 20:11, Psalm 33:6, Jeremiah 32:17, Colossians 1:16

CONSIDER

What's significant about the first dozen words in scripture? And what's so important about the creation stories in Genesis 1 and 2? They tell us who God is, how the universe got here, and how God made us in His own likeness. Scientists can study, but it all comes back to God. Knowing God is our Creator makes sense of everything else that follows.

PONDER

* What thrills you most in God's creation? When was the last time you enjoyed that?

* What difference does it make that the Lord is your Creator and Maker?

* Take a minute right now to thank God for forming you and breathing His life into you.

More about The Lord God Created All Things: 2 Kings 19:15, Psalm 121:2, John 1:3, Romans 1:20, 1 Corinthians 8:5–6, Hebrews 1:2

Day 27

God Is Without Beginning or End

THE BIBLE SAYS

Lord, You have been the place of comfort for all people of all time. Before the mountains were born, before You gave birth to the earth and the world, forever and ever, You are God.

The Lord rules. He is dressed with great power. The Lord has dressed Himself with strength. For sure, the world is built to last. It will not be moved. Your throne is set up from long ago. You have always been.

You made the earth in the beginning. You made the heavens with Your hands. . . . And they will be changed, but You are always the same. Your years will never end.

The God Who lives forever is the Lord, the One Who made the ends of the earth.

We give honor and thanks to the King Who lives forever. He is the One Who never dies.

Bible References: Psalm 90:1–2, Psalm 93:1–2, Psalm 102:25–27, Isaiah 40:28, 1 Timothy 1:17

CONSIDER

Thanks to the diligent work of thousands of astrophysicists working in scores of locations around the world, we're learning more about the universe every year. Essentially, every year the universe appears more complex, more paradoxical, and more designed. During the writing of this book, they announced that the universe is finite. Indeed, only God is infinite and eternal, without beginning or end. What a mighty God we serve!

PONDER

* What are the implications if God is without beginning?

* What are the implications if God is without end?

* What are the implications of receiving eternal life?

More about God Is Without Beginning or End: Genesis 21:33, Isaiah 41:4, Isaiah 44:6, Isaiah 48:12, Micah 5:2

Day 28

God Is Always Good

THE BIBLE SAYS

"O give thanks to the Lord, for He is good. His loving-kindness lasts forever."

O taste and see that the Lord is good. How happy is the man who trusts in Him! O fear the Lord, all you who belong to Him. For those who fear Him never want for anything.

For You are good and ready to forgive, O Lord. You are rich in loving-kindness to all who call to You.

The Lord is good, a safe place in times of trouble. And He knows those who come to Him to be safe.

We know that God makes all things work together for the good of those who love Him and are chosen to be a part of His plan.

Bible References: 1 Chronicles 16:34, Psalm 34:8–9, Psalm 86:5, Nahum 1:7, Romans 8:28

CONSIDER

The first chapter of the Bible says nine times that each thing God created was "good." It was good because God Himself is good. He is always and infinitely good. There is nothing bad, defective, or not right about who He is. He is good through and through—yesterday, today, and forever. Therefore, we can trust His heart. He is good, indeed!

PONDER

* How many friends of yours have a genuinely good heart?

* What clues tell you that each friend has a genuinely good heart?

* What does the Bible say about God's thoroughly good heart?

More about God Is Always Good: Psalm 25:8, Psalm 31:19, Psalm 35:28, Psalm 92:15, Psalm 129:4, Psalm 135:3, Psalm 136:1–9, Matthew 19:17, 1 Peter 2:9, 2 Peter 1:3

Day 29

God Wants Us to Be Holy

THE BIBLE SAYS

"Do not keep from doing what is right and fair in trying to help a poor brother when he has a problem."

Be right and fair in what you decide. Stand up for the rights of those who are suffering and in need.

"Learn to do good. Look for what is right and fair."

You are to shine as lights among the sinful people of this world.

Show other Christians how to live by your life. They should be able to follow you in the way you talk and in what you do. Show them how to live in faith and in love and in holy living.

Bible References: Exodus 23:6, Proverbs 31:9, Isaiah 1:17, Philippians 2:15, 1 Timothy 4:12

CONSIDER

Holy isn't what most women aspire to be—it sounds outdated and artificial. But God wants you and me to be pure, clean, good, and holy in His sight. Not to look good but to be like Him. He wants us to treat others well. Not out of pride or self-sabotage but out of who God made us to be because we belong to Jesus. This is true in every circumstance, situation, and sphere of life.

PONDER

* Why is it harder to be holy in our private lives?

* Why is it a waste to try to act good out of pride?

* Ask God to empower you to do good for His glory.

More about God Wants Us to Be Holy: Genesis 18:19, Deuteronomy 16:19–20, Deuteronomy 24:17, 2 Samuel 22:27, Ezekiel 36:25, John 13:4–10, 1 Corinthians 5:8, 2 Corinthians 7:1, Ephesians 5:25–27

Day 30

God Wants Everyone to Be Sorry

THE BIBLE SAYS

"I am not pleased with the death of anyone who dies," says the Lord God. "So be sorry for your sins and turn away from them, and live."

"Yet from this day on I will bring good to you."

You know that God is kind. He is trying to get you to be sorry for your sins and turn from them.

He wants all people to be saved from the punishment of sin. He wants them to come to know the truth.

The Lord does not want any person to be punished forever. He wants all people to be sorry for their sins and turn from them.

Bible References: Ezekiel 18:32, Haggai 2:19, Romans 2:4, 1 Timothy 2:4, 2 Peter 3:9

CONSIDER

God loves us and wants what's best for us in this life and forever. When God urges people to be sorry for sin, it isn't because He is nursing His pride or needing our apology. He knows that the only way we can escape the pain and punishment of our sin is to be sorry and experience His forgiveness. God is passionate for each person to escape death and experience life abundant now and forever.

PONDER

* God wants everyone to be sorry for their sins. Why?

* Ultimately, what does God want everyone to enjoy?

* Have you experienced Jesus' forgiveness after you were sorry for your sins?

More about God Wants Everyone to Be Sorry: Exodus 34:5–9, Deuteronomy 30:15–19, Isaiah 48:9, Jeremiah 36:3, Ezekiel 18:23, Ezekiel 33:11, Jonah 3:10

Still more: Matthew 18:14, Luke 7:38–50, Luke 21:18, John 3:16, John 10:28, 1 Timothy 1:16

Day 31

God Is Loving and Shows Pity

THE BIBLE SAYS

"I will have loving-kindness and loving-pity for anyone I want to."

Remember Your loving-pity and Your loving-kindness, O Lord. For they have been from old.

O God, favor me because of Your loving-kindness. Take away my wrong-doing because of the greatness of Your loving-pity.

"With loving-kindness that lasts forever I will have pity on you," says the Lord Who bought you and saves you.

[Jesus:] "The son got up and went to his father. While he was yet a long way off, his father saw him. The father was full of loving-pity for him. He ran and threw his arms around him and kissed him."

Bible References: Exodus 33:19, Psalm 25:6, Psalm 51:1, Isaiah 54:8, Luke 15:20

CONSIDER

Nearly two thousand years ago, Jesus told the story

about a rebellious son and a loving father. The story never gets old. When the son came home, the father responded in the most loving-kind way possible. He welcomed his son back by running to him, throwing his arms around him, kissing him, and celebrating with a big party that very evening.

The father didn't even let his son finish his carefully worded apology. All was forgiven long before that day.

Likewise, God wants to show His loving-pity and loving-kindness to you and me. What a great heavenly Father in every way. We can depend on that extravagant loving response from Him every time.

PONDER

* Why is God quick to forgive us?

* Why is God quick to lavish good gifts on us?

* Why does heaven celebrate when someone turns to Him?

More about God Is Loving and Shows Pity: Deuteronomy 13:17, Psalm 103:13, Psalm 145:9, Isaiah 30:18, Isaiah 49:13

God Is Slow to Anger

THE BIBLE SAYS

"But now, I pray, let the power of the Lord be great as You have promised, saying, 'The Lord is slow to anger and filled with loving-kindness, forgiving sin and wrong-doing.' "

You, O Lord, are a God full of love and pity. You are slow to anger and rich in loving-kindness and truth.

Return to the Lord your God, for He is full of loving-kindness and loving-pity. He is slow to anger, full of love, and ready to keep His punishment from you.

"I knew that You are slow to anger and are filled with loving-kindness, always ready to change Your mind and not punish."

The Lord is slow to anger and great in power.

Bible References: Numbers 14:17–18, Psalm 86:15, Joel 2:13, Jonah 4:2, Nahum 1:3

CONSIDER

Would you consider yourself quick or slow to get angry? What about the family you grew up in or the people you live with now? Living with an angry person keeps you on edge. The old preachers repeatedly describe God as slow to get angry. God doesn't have the triggers and sore spots people do. We don't need to tiptoe around the Lord, fearful He is about to explode. His anger is at sin, and He can wait as long as it takes to help us be sorry and come to Him. He even continues to wait to judge the world.

PONDER

* When was the last time you got angry? What pushed your buttons?

* How do you compare your anger to God's anger? Any differences?

* What would be different if God wasn't slow to anger?

More about God Is Slow to Anger: Exodus 34:6, Nehemiah 9:17, Psalm 103:8, Psalm 145:8, Jeremiah 15:15

Day 33

In This Life, All Have Sinned

THE BIBLE SAYS

"There is no man who does not sin."

For sure there is not a right and good man on earth who always does good and never sins.

The Holy Writings say, "There is not one person who is right with God. No, not even one!"

All men have sinned.

If we say that we have no sin, we lie to ourselves and the truth is not in us.

Bible References: 1 Kings 8:46, Ecclesiastes 7:20, Romans 3:10, Romans 3:23, 1 John 1:8

CONSIDER

You probably think of yourself as a good person but not perfect. Most women have a sense of not measuring up. But we've all missed the mark. We've all sinned. A lot. That's why God is so intent on making us new—new creations, reborn, born again, born from above. We'll consider more about that good news over the next two days.

PONDER

* What would you consider sinful about your actions and attitudes?

* Whom do you measure yourself against?

* Can you agree when God says everyone has sinned? Why or why not?

More about In This Life, All Have Sinned: 2 Chronicles 6:36, Psalm 14:1-3, Psalm 53:1, Psalm 143:2, Proverbs 20:9, Ecclesiastes 7:29, Isaiah 59:4-8, Isaiah 64:6, Jeremiah 2:9, Jeremiah 5:1-9, Jeremiah 6:28, Jeremiah 17:9, Micah 7:2

Still more: Matthew 15:19, Isaiah 53:6, Romans 8:7, Galatians 5:19-21, Ephesians 2:1-2, Ephesians 6:12, Colossians 3:5-7, Titus 3:3, James 3:2, 1 John 2:15-16, 1 John 3:8, 1 John 3:10, Revelation 21:4

Day 34

Only God Can Make Us New (1 of 2)

THE BIBLE SAYS

The gifts on an altar that God wants are a broken spirit. O God, You will not hate a broken heart and a heart with no pride.

[Jesus:] "If one sinner is sorry for his sins and turns from them, the angels are very happy."

[Jesus:] "Men must be sorry for their sins and turn from them. Then they will be forgiven."

You get what is coming to you when you sin. It is death! But God's free gift is life that lasts forever. It is given to us by our Lord Jesus Christ.

Let us thank the God and Father of our Lord Jesus Christ. It was through His loving-kindness that we were born again to a new life and have a hope that never dies. This hope is ours because Jesus was raised from the dead.

Bible References: Psalm 51:17, Luke 15:10, Luke 24:47, Romans 6:23, 1 Peter 1:3

CONSIDER

We are saved by God's loving-kindness and loving-favor, forgiven and made clean in His sight. Only God can make us new like that. All He asks is that we're sorry for our sins, turn from them, turn to God, and ask to be forgiven. He does the rest. What good news, indeed!

PONDER

* What is God's plan for dealing with our guilt and sin?

* What do we stand to lose by confessing our sins to God?

* Have you received God's gift of new life? How and when?

More about Only God Can Make Us New: Genesis 19:16, Luke 18:13, John 3:36, Romans 6:14, 2 Corinthians 4:15, Ephesians 2:5, Ephesians 2:8–9, Titus 3:5

Day 35

Only God Can Make Us New (2 of 2)

THE BIBLE SAYS

"You are all beautiful, my love. You are perfect."

[Jesus:] "Those who have a pure heart are happy, because they will see God."

Christ made us right with God and set us apart for God and made us holy. Christ bought us with His blood and made us free from our sins.

Our sins are washed away and we are made clean because Christ gave His own body as a gift to God. He did this once for all time.

You have been given a new birth. It was from a seed that cannot die. This new life is from the Word of God which lives forever.

Bible References: Song of Solomon 4:7, Matthew 5:8, 1 Corinthians 1:30, Hebrews 10:10, 1 Peter 1:23

CONSIDER

Yesterday we saw how we are saved by God's loving-kindness and loving-favor, forgiven and made clean in His sight. Those of us who are saved and made holy by God are adopted into His family. This new life certainly isn't trouble-free this side of heaven. Yet who we are, whose we are, what we are, and what is true for us now and in the future—it's all changed for the best!

PONDER

* If God told an angel about you, would He say you're new—or not yet?

* How can God honestly say someone is beautiful, perfect, and pure?

* How can God say someone's sins are washed away forever?

More about Only God Can Make Us New: Psalm 15:1–5, John 1:12–13, John 3:3–7, Ephesians 1:4–5, Ephesians 5:25–27, Colossians 1:19–22, 1 Thessalonians 3:13, Hebrews 10:22, Hebrews 13:12, 1 John 3:9, 1 John 4:7

Day 36

Ask God to Make You New Today!

THE BIBLE SAYS

Let him turn to the Lord, and He will have loving-pity on him. Let him turn to our God, for He will for sure forgive all his sins.

"As for the proud one, his soul is not right in him. But the one who is right and good will live by his faith."

He said, "Sirs, what must I do to be saved?" They said, "Put your trust in the Lord Jesus Christ."

The Holy Writings say, "I heard you at the right time. I helped you on that day to be saved from the punishment of sin. Now is the right time! See! Now is the day to be saved."

The Word of the Lord will last forever. That Word is the Good News which was preached to you.

Bible References: Isaiah 55:7, Habakkuk 2:4, Acts 16:30–31, 2 Corinthians 6:2, 1 Peter 1:25

CONSIDER

How good that we can thank the Lord daily for Jesus

Christ's perfect life, death on the cross, burial, and resurrection from the dead on the third day. He did all that to offer the best good news the world has ever heard. Have you believed it yet? If you're not sure, make sure right now!

PONDER

* Pray: "Heavenly Father, thank You for offering to forgive me and make me new."

* Pray: "Thank You for sending Your Son, Jesus, to die for my sins and offer me new, eternal life."

* Pray: "I admit my sins, I confess Jesus as my Lord, and I gladly receive Your salvation now."

More about Ask God to Make You New Today!: Isaiah 55:1-6, Matthew 19:16, Luke 10:40-42, John 6:27, 2 Corinthians 4:18, Hebrews 12:16

Day 37

Light versus Darkness

THE BIBLE SAYS

Then God said, "Let there be light," and there was light. God saw that the light was good. He divided the light from the darkness. Then God called the light day, and He called the darkness night. There was evening and there was morning, one day.

"For You are my lamp, O Lord. The Lord gives light to my darkness."

The Lord is my light and the One Who saves me. Whom should I fear? The Lord is the strength of my life. Of whom should I be afraid?

I looked on the earth and saw that it was an empty waste. I looked to the heavens, and they had no light.

[Jesus:] "The man who does what is right comes to the Light. What he does will be seen because he has done what God wanted him to do."

Bible References: Genesis 1:3–5, 2 Samuel 22:29, Psalm 27:1, Jeremiah 4:23, John 3:21

CONSIDER

Light triumphs over darkness. The two cannot coexist. Light *always* wins.

God's Son, Jesus, is the Light of the World. Where He is, the darkness of evil cannot be. And where His Spirit dwells, darkness evaporates.

If you have accepted the grace of Jesus and made Him the Lord and light of your life, His powerful, all-encompassing shining-greatness and beautiful light live inside you.

PONDER

* Why do you think God chose light to represent Himself?

* Have you ever been stuck in the dark? How did you feel when the lights came back on?

* How have you seen God's light dispel darkness in your life?

More about Light versus Darkness: Leviticus 24:1–4, Job 24:13–17, Job 38:8–20, 1 John 1:5–8

Day 38

Jesus Is the Light

THE BIBLE SAYS

This true Light, coming into the world, gives light to every man.

[Jesus:] "The Light has come into the world. And the Light is the test by which men are guilty or not. People love darkness more than the Light because the things they do are sinful."

Jesus spoke to all the people, saying, "I am the Light of the world. Anyone who follows Me will not walk in darkness. He will have the Light of Life."

[Jesus:] "While I am in the world, I am the Light of the world."

[Jesus:] "While you have the Light, put your trust in the Light. Then you will be the sons of the Light."

Bible References: John 1:9, John 3:19, John 8:12, John 9:5, John 12:36

CONSIDER

Even today, Jesus Christ's light shines heaven's almighty power against the terrible power, evil, and wickedness of Satan's dark and doomed kingdom. When we believe that Jesus died for all the sins of the world and when we forgive others, we shine the light of the Gospel even farther and we refute Satan's deadly agenda. No wonder Jesus told His disciples, "You [too] are the light of the world" (Matthew 5:14).

PONDER

* How are you and other Christians the light of the world?

* What does it take for Jesus Christ's light to shine through you?

* What can His light through you do to bring light and change to other people?

More about Jesus Is the Light: Isaiah 49:6, John 11:9, Acts 13:47, 2 Corinthians 4:4–6, Revelation 22:5

Still more: Exodus 4:11, Psalm 146:8, Isaiah 29:18, Isaiah 35:5, Isaiah 42:7,

Day 39

Jesus Christ: True God, True Man

THE BIBLE SAYS

The birth of Jesus Christ was like this: Mary His mother had been promised in marriage to Joseph. Before they were married, it was learned that she was to have a baby by the Holy Spirit.

Jesus was about thirty years old when He began His work. People thought Jesus was the son of Joseph.

Christ became human flesh and lived among us. We saw His shining-greatness. This greatness is given only to a much-loved Son from His Father. He was full of loving-favor and truth.

Christ came to earth as a Man. He was pure in His Spirit. He was seen by angels. The nations heard about Him. Men everywhere put their trust in Him. He was taken up into heaven.

Christ is the Word of Life. He was from the beginning. We have heard Him and have seen Him with our own eyes. We have looked at Him and put our hands on Him.

Bible References: Matthew 1:18, Luke 3:23, John 1:14, 1 Timothy 3:16, 1 John 1:1

CONSIDER

Jesus, God's Son, was born human and lived here on earth for more than thirty years. Without question, Jesus was and is true God—He didn't change who He was. Yet Jesus chose to become a true man as well. It's a mystery that continues even now that Jesus is in heaven.

PONDER

* Why do you think Jesus didn't just appear as a full-grown man?

* Why do you think Jesus waited thirty years to begin His public ministry?

* What does it matter that Jesus became human and still remained God?

More about Jesus Christ: True God, True Man: John 1:1–18, Philippians 2:6–11, Colossians 1:15–16, Hebrews 1:1–3, Hebrews 2:14

Day 40

For Our Sakes, Jesus Was Poor

THE BIBLE SAYS

Jesus said to him, "Foxes have holes. Birds have nests. But the Son of Man has no place to lay His head."

[Jesus:] "The Spirit of the Lord is on Me. He has put His hand on Me to preach the Good News to poor people."

[Jesus] looked at His followers and said, "Those of you who are poor are happy, because the holy nation of God is yours."

[Jesus:] "Poor people have the Good News preached to them."

You know of the loving-favor shown by our Lord Jesus Christ. He was rich, but He became poor for your good. In that way, because He became poor, you might become rich.

Bible References: Matthew 8:20, Luke 4:18, Luke 6:20, Luke 7:22, 2 Corinthians 8:9

CONSIDER

Jesus and His followers preached the Gospel and quietly gave money to the poor. The Lord didn't just watch the poor widow give her last two mites. He likely sent a disciple with silver coins to meet her pressing needs. Then again, we often forget that Jesus Himself spent the better part of three years depending on the charity of others. Except for the generosity of others, Jesus was earthly poor. He wanted it that way.

PONDER

* Why do you think Jesus chose to be earthly poor "for your good"?

* What do you think the followers of Jesus gained from His example?

* What does it mean that "He became poor, [that] you might become rich"?

More about For Our Sakes, Jesus Was Poor: Matthew 5:3, Matthew 11:5, Luke 4:18, Luke 7:22, Luke 8:1–3, Luke 9:58, John 12:5, Philippians 4:10–20

Day 41

Jesus Christ Proclaimed Good News

THE BIBLE SAYS

From that time on, Jesus went about preaching. He said, "Be sorry for your sins and turn from them. The holy nation of heaven is near."

Jesus went over all Galilee. He taught in their places of worship and preached the Good News of the holy nation. He healed all kinds of sickness and disease among the people.

Jesus went on to all the towns and cities. He taught in their places of worship. He preached the Good News of the holy nation of God. He healed every sickness and disease the people had.

After John the Baptist was put in prison, Jesus came to the country of Galilee. He preached the Good News of God.

[Jesus] said to them, "I must preach about the holy nation of God in other cities also. This is why I was sent."

Bible References: Matthew 4:17, Matthew 4:23, Matthew 9:35, Mark 1:14, Luke 4:43

CONSIDER

Jesus lived out His life in Nazareth—until He started preaching the Good News. Then Jesus gave up His home and became a traveling teacher. He didn't always go where people wanted or expected Him to go, but He went exactly where He knew people would hear and some would receive Him.

PONDER

* What motivated Jesus to leave His home and become a traveling preacher?

* How would you have reacted to Jesus coming to your city or town?

* How have you responded to Jesus' message of Good News?

More about Jesus Christ Proclaimed Good News: Luke 4:18, Luke 20:1, John 3:16, John 3:36, John 5:24, John 6:40, John 11:25–26, John 20:31, John 21:31

Day 42

Jesus Christ Forgives Our Sins

THE BIBLE SAYS

[Jesus:] "The Son of Man has power on earth to forgive sins."

[Jesus] said to the woman, "Your sins are forgiven." Those who were eating with Him began to say to themselves, "Who is this Man Who even forgives sins?" He said to the woman, "Your faith has saved you from the punishment of sin. Go in peace."

[Jesus:] "For sure, I tell you, anyone who hears My Word and puts his trust in Him Who sent Me has life that lasts forever. He will not be guilty. He has already passed from death into life."

"All the early preachers spoke of this. Everyone who puts his trust in Christ will have his sins forgiven through His name."

But now God proves that He is right in saving men from sin. He shows that He is the One Who has no sin. God makes anyone right with Himself who puts his trust in Jesus.

Bible References: Matthew 9:6, Luke 7:48–50, John 5:24, Acts 10:43, Romans 3:26

CONSIDER

God the Father forgives sins. As God the Son, Jesus also has the authority to forgive sins. Jesus forgives the sins of all who trust Him for new life. When Jesus forgives sins, God the Father forgives them too. They always work in harmony.

PONDER

* When did God decide to forgive our sins?

* What gives Jesus the authority and ability to forgive our sins?

* How do you experience God's forgiveness?

More about Jesus Christ Forgives Our Sins: Mark 2:3–12, Acts 5:31, Acts 13:38, Hebrews 12:24, 1 John 5:13

Day 43

Jesus Christ Died for Our Sins

THE BIBLE SAYS

[Jesus] Himself carried the sin of many, and prayed for the sinners.

[Jesus:] "For the Son of Man did not come to be cared for. He came to care for others. He came to give His life so that many could be bought by His blood and be made free from sin."

God will make us right with Himself. . .if we put our trust in God Who raised Jesus our Lord from the dead.

First of all, I taught you what I had received. It was this: Christ died for our sins as the Holy Writings said He would. Christ was buried. He was raised from the dead three days later as the Holy Writings said He would.

[Jesus] carried our sins in His own body when He died on a cross. In doing this, we may be dead to sin and alive to all that is right and good. His wounds have healed you!

Bible References: Isaiah 53:12, Mark 10:45, Romans 4:24, 1 Corinthians 15:3–4, 1 Peter 2:24

CONSIDER

What is the Good News? The Gospel message is this: Jesus is God's Son. He lived a perfect life here on earth. Even though He had committed no sin, Jesus was nailed to a Roman cross. Jesus died in our place for our sins. He was buried late that same afternoon. On the third day, Jesus rose from the dead. He proved that our sins really are forgiven!

PONDER

* Jesus died for us.

* Jesus died for our sins.

* Jesus died for the sins of the whole world.

More about Jesus Christ Died for Our Sins: Isaiah 53:8–9, Matthew 27:60, Mark 15:46–47, Luke 23:53, John 19:42, 1 John 2:2

Day 44

Jesus Christ Rose from the Dead

THE BIBLE SAYS

From that time on Jesus began to tell His followers that He had to go to Jerusalem and suffer many things.... He told them He would be killed and three days later He would be raised from the dead.

"He is not here! He has risen from the dead as He said He would."

"God raised [Jesus] to life on the third day and made Him to be seen."

If you say with your mouth that Jesus is Lord, and believe in your heart that God raised Him from the dead, you will be saved from the punishment of sin.

[Jesus] was raised from the dead three days later as the Holy Writings said He would.

Bible References: Matthew 16:21, Matthew 28:6, Acts 10:40, Romans 10:9, 1 Corinthians 15:4

CONSIDER

When a loved one passes away, we know we won't see him or her again in this life. Death doesn't budge. But Jesus, Creator of life, stronger than death, physically rose from the dead. Jesus ate food, and His disciples touched His physical resurrected body. For forty days, Jesus appeared to His followers before He returned to God in heaven. He remains alive for eternity!

PONDER

* Jesus' followers grieved and Satan rejoiced when Jesus died. What did everyone forget?

* How did Jesus prove He was really alive from the dead?

* How easy or hard is it to believe that Jesus was dead but is now alive forever?

More about Jesus Christ Rose from the Dead: Matthew 28:16, Mark 16:5-6, Luke 24:5-8, Luke 24:13-15, Luke 24:34, Luke 24:36, Luke 24:39-40, Luke 24:44-46, John 20:19-20, John 20:26, John 21:1, Acts 13:37

Day 45

Jesus Brings Us into God's Forever Family (1 of 2)

THE BIBLE SAYS

[Jesus] came to His own, but His own did not receive Him. He gave the right and the power to become children of God to those who received Him. He gave this to those who put their trust in His name.

God knew from the beginning who would put their trust in Him. So He chose them and made them to be like His Son. Christ was first and all those who belong to God are His brothers.

"I will be a Father to you. You will be My sons and daughters, says the All-powerful God."

You are now children of God because you have put your trust in Christ Jesus.

God already planned to have us as His own children. This was done by Jesus Christ. In His plan God wanted this done.

Bible References: John 1:11–12, Romans 8:29, 2 Corinthians 6:18, Galatians 3:26, Ephesians 1:5

CONSIDER

We didn't choose the family we are born into, even though that one factor determines so much about our lives. But Jesus gives the right to become children of God to anyone who receives Him and trusts in Him. We get to say yes to being in God's eternal family. When we do, the Lord changes our family, identity, and whole life here and now—and for eternity.

PONDER

* What, if anything, made it hard for you to receive Jesus Christ?

* Why would anyone *not* want to become a child of God?

* How do you experience being a child of God?

More about Jesus Brings Us into God's Forever Family: John 14:6, Romans 8:14–15, Ephesians 2:19, Ephesians 5:1, Hebrews 2:10, 1 John 3:1–3

Day 46

Jesus Brings Us into God's Forever Family (2 of 2)

THE BIBLE SAYS

[Jesus:] "Whoever does what My father in heaven wants him to do is My brother and My sister and My mother."

[Jesus:] "Anyone who lives and has put his trust in Me will never die. Do you believe this?"

Jesus said, "I am the Way and the Truth and the Life. No one can go to the Father except by Me."

Jesus makes men holy. He takes away their sins. Both Jesus and the ones being made holy have the same Father. That is why Jesus is not ashamed to call them His brothers.

The one who says he knows the Son has the Father also.

Bible References: Matthew 12:50, John 11:26, John 14:6, Hebrews 2:11, 1 John 2:23

CONSIDER

The forgiveness of all our sins, adoption into God's

family, eternal life, and salvation are all found in Jesus Christ alone. When we believe in and receive Jesus, we not only come to know God's Son, but we also come to know God our heavenly Father. We also receive the Holy Spirit, who permanently lives within every Christian. In other words, the Trinity embraces us. What a wonderful family in every way!

PONDER

* How does it feel to know the Trinity embraces you?

* What's the best thing about being part of God's family now?

* What newfound joys might you experience some-day in heaven?

More about Jesus Brings Us into God's Forever Family: John 10:7, Acts 4:12, Romans 10:8–10, Romans 10:13, Romans 10:17, 1 Timothy 1:16

Day 47

God Loves You!

THE BIBLE SAYS

[Jesus:] "For God so loved the world that He gave His only Son. Whoever puts his trust in God's Son will not be lost but will have life that lasts forever."

No one is willing to die for another person, but for a good man someone might be willing to die. But God showed His love to us. While we were still sinners, Christ died for us.

Even before the world was made, God chose us for Himself because of His love. He planned that we should be holy and without blame as He sees us.

God has chosen you. You are holy and loved by Him.

Keep yourselves in the love of God. Wait for life that lasts forever through the loving-kindness of our Lord Jesus Christ.

Bible References: John 3:16, Romans 5:7–8, Ephesians 1:4, Colossians 3:12, Jude 21

CONSIDER

Even on your worst day, God is never angry or mad at you. If you think God is furious at you, Satan is lying to you again. The truth is Jesus took care of all punishment once and for all. The truth is that the Lord is crazy about you, as He always has been. And now you *belong* to Him. Satan's lies put a black cloud over our heads. Instead, God's love changes everything!

PONDER

* ✳ How often do you feel God is mad at you?

* ✳ How often do you feel God is crazy in love with you?

* ✳ What makes the difference?

More about God Loves You!: Romans 10:38–39, Ephesians 2:4, 2 Thessalonians 2:16, Titus 3:4–5, 1 John 4:7–12

Day 48

Don't Be Discouraged: God Is with You!

THE BIBLE SAYS

"Be strong and have strength of heart. . . . For the Lord your God is the One Who goes with you. He will be faithful to you. He will not leave you alone."

"Have I not told you? Be strong and have strength of heart! Do not be afraid or lose faith. For the Lord your God is with you anywhere you go."

The Lord is my strength and my safe cover. My heart trusts in Him, and I am helped. So my heart is full of joy. I will thank Him with my song.

[Jesus:] "I am with you always, even to the end of the world."

God has said, "I will never leave you or let you be alone."

Bible References: Deuteronomy 31:6, Joshua 1:9, Psalm 28:7, Matthew 28:20, Hebrews 13:5

CONSIDER

Once you're part of God's family, He is with you always—and will be forever. He will never leave you on your own. In part, that's why the Lord sent His Holy Spirit to live within you. His Holy Spirit gives you all the strength and courage and joy and peace you need to face today's challenges and tomorrow's uncertainties. God the Father will never leave you. Jesus Himself is always with you. And the Holy Spirit is staying put inside you as well. Be encouraged!

PONDER

* God gives you all the power, protection, provision, and peace you need.

* Jesus set the example by always listening to His Father and doing His will.

* The Holy Spirit offers you His counsel, comfort, and encouragement always.

More about Don't Be Discouraged: God Is with You!: Psalm 10:17, Psalm 73:25–26, Daniel 10:19, John 14:16–17, Philippians 4:9

Day 49

The Holy Spirit Lives in Us

THE BIBLE SAYS

They were all filled with the Holy Spirit.

"God says, 'In the last days I will send My Spirit on all men.'"

No one belongs to Christ if he does not have Christ's Spirit in him.

[God] has put His mark on us to show we belong to Him. His Spirit is in our hearts to prove this.

The truth is the Good News. When you heard the truth, you put your trust in Christ. Then God marked you by giving you His Holy Spirit as a promise.

[God] has given us His Spirit. This is how we live by His help and He lives in us.

Bible References: Acts 2:4, Acts 2:17, Romans 8:9, 2 Corinthians 1:22, Ephesians 1:13, 1 John 4:13

CONSIDER

The early preacher Moses dreamed of the day when

all God's people would receive His Holy Spirit. That dream became reality a few days after Jesus ascended back to heaven. He sent His Holy Spirit to live within every Christian. And not just temporarily but always. What an immense gift to receive, cherish, and enjoy forever. God isn't just with you. He's inside you!

PONDER

* Take a moment to consider that you are not the only one living inside your body.

* How does it feel to know you are never alone, never without God's presence?

* Express your love and deep gratitude to the Holy Spirit.

More about The Holy Spirit Lives in Us: John 7:37–39, Acts 10:45, 1 Corinthians 2:12, 1 Corinthians 3:16–17, Galatians 3:2, Titus 3:5–6, 1 John 3:24

Day 50

Pray in the Power of the Spirit

THE BIBLE SAYS

"I will pour out the Spirit of loving-favor and prayer on the family of David and on those who live in Jerusalem."

When they had finished praying, the place where they were gathered was shaken. They were all filled with the Holy Spirit. It was easy for them to speak the Word of God.

In the same way, the Holy Spirit helps us where we are weak. We do not know how to pray or what we should pray for, but the Holy Spirit prays to God for us with sounds that cannot be put into words.

I pray that because of the riches of His shining-greatness, He will make you strong with power in your hearts through the Holy Spirit.

Dear friends, you must become strong in your most holy faith. Let the Holy Spirit lead you as you pray.

Bible References: Zechariah 12:10, Acts 4:31, Romans 8:26, Ephesians 3:16, Jude 20

CONSIDER

We ask others to pray for us. Have you ever thought about how the Holy Spirit prays for you? When you don't know how to pray, the Holy Spirit inside you prays for you with heartfelt sounds way beyond words. The Father knows exactly what the Spirit is asking and gladly says yes. Do you ever feel your prayers are weak? Never forget the Holy Spirit empowers those prayers!

PONDER

* The Holy Spirit's languages exceed anything human or angelic.

* The Holy Spirit's power is infinite. He never gets weary or tired.

* The Spirit's knowledge is infinite. He knows exactly what to pray.

More about Pray in the Power of the Spirit: Matthew 26:41, Mark 14:38, Luke 10:21, Luke 22:44, Romans 15:13, Romans 15:30

Day 51

Prayer Makes a Difference!

THE BIBLE SAYS

[Jesus:] "I say to you who hear Me, love those who work against you. Do good to those who hate you. Respect and give thanks for those who try to bring bad to you. Pray for those who make it very hard for you."

You must pray at all times as the Holy Spirit leads you to pray. Pray for the things that are needed. You must watch and keep on praying. Remember to pray for all Christians. Pray for me also. Pray that I might open my mouth without fear.

Because of your prayers and the help the Holy Spirit gives me, all of this will turn out for good.

First of all, I ask you to pray much for all men and to give thanks for them.

The prayer from the heart of a man right with God has much power.

Bible References: Luke 6:27–28, Ephesians 6:18–19, Philippians 1:19, 1 Timothy 2:1, James 5:16

CONSIDER

In Ephesians 6, Paul urges us to pray for all Christians. In 1 Timothy 2, he urges us to pray for all people. In other words, we can and should pray for Christians and not-yet-Christians alike. In both cases, prayer makes a difference!

PONDER

* God asks us to pray, so of course He wants to hear our requests!

* Our Father always hears the prayers of family and friends and delights to answer their prayers, just as He delights to answer yours.

* If you think prayer doesn't make a difference, talk to others who pray and know God answers.

More about Prayer Makes a Difference!: Genesis 20:17, Deuteronomy 9:20, Psalm 55:17, Matthew 5:44, Colossians 4:3, 2 Thessalonians 3:2, 1 Timothy 2:2–4, 1 Peter 3:12

Day 52

Worship the True God Alone

THE BIBLE SAYS

"Follow the Lord your God and fear Him. Keep His Laws, and listen to His voice. Work for Him, and hold on to Him."

"So fear the Lord. Serve Him in faith and truth."

Jesus said to the devil, "Get away, Satan. It is written, 'You must worship the Lord your God. You must obey Him only.'"

[Jesus:] "This is life that lasts forever. It is to know You, the only true God, and to know Jesus Christ Whom You have sent."

We are joined together with the true God through His Son, Jesus Christ.

Bible References: Deuteronomy 13:4, Joshua 24:14, Matthew 4:10, John 17:3, 1 John 5:20

CONSIDER

The Bible says we're to fear, honor, praise, and worship

the Lord God alone. Does it sound easy? It's not. The world, the flesh, and the devil try their best to get us to worship anything, *anything,* but the one true God. The fact is you *can* worship anything. Don't! It will poison your heart, soul, mind, and strength. It will ruin your relationships with others. Give God the worship of your heart and life; He is the only one who deserves it.

PONDER

* What responsibilities, dreams, or desires keep you from giving yourself completely to God?

* What lies does Satan tell you in order to draw you away from worshipping God alone?

* Take a moment and come to God in worship. Tell Him you love Him, you serve Him, and He is your all in all.

More about Worship the True God Alone: Genesis 4:26, Deuteronomy 10:20, 2 Kings 17:36, Isaiah 26:13, Mark 12:32, 1 Corinthians 8:4–6, Ephesians 4:6, 1 Timothy 2:5, Revelation 15:4

Day 53

Praise God by Saying, "Let It Be So"

THE BIBLE SAYS

" 'Honor be to the Lord, the God of Israel forever and ever.' " Then all the people said, "Let it be so!"

All the people said, "Let it be so!" and praised the Lord.

Then Ezra gave honor and thanks to the Lord the great God. And all the people answered, "Let it be so!"

Honor be to the Lord, the God of Israel, forever and ever! Let it be so!

Honor and thanks be to the Lord, the God of Israel, forever and ever. Let all the people say, "Let it be so!"

Bible References: 1 Chronicles 16:36, Nehemiah 5:13, Nehemiah 8:6, Psalm 41:13, Psalm 106:48

CONSIDER

When it comes to God's honor and praise, the Bible frequently says, "Let it be so!" It's like echoing a refrain, standing in applause, asking for an encore. What we hear, say, and repeat goes deeply into our souls.

May we cultivate a heart attitude and habit of hearing God's Word and saying, "Let it be so!"

PONDER

* Let's honor, praise, and worship the one true God alone. Let it be so!

* Let's thank the Lord God for His many gifts to us in this life. Let it be so!

* Let's look forward to being with the Lord in His presence forever. Let it be so!

More about Praise God by Saying, "Let It Be So": Psalm 72:19, Psalm 89:52, Romans 1:25, Romans 9:5, Romans 11:36, Romans 15:33, Romans 16:27

Still more: Galatians 1:5, Philippians 4:20, 1 Timothy 1:17, 1 Timothy 6:16, 2 Timothy 4:18, Hebrews 13:21, 1 Peter 4:11, 1 Peter 5:11, 2 Peter 3:18, Jude 25

Day 54

Praising God Isn't Always Expressive

THE BIBLE SAYS

The Lord is my Shepherd. I will have everything I need. He lets me rest in fields of green grass. He leads me beside the quiet waters.

Rest in the Lord and be willing to wait for Him.

Be quiet and know that I am God. I will be honored among the nations. I will be honored in the earth.

Be quiet before the Lord God!

[Jesus:] "Come to Me, all of you who work and have heavy loads. I will give you rest. Follow My teachings and learn from Me. I am gentle and do not have pride. You will have rest for your souls."

Bible References: Psalm 23:1–2, Psalm 37:7, Psalm 46:10, Zephaniah 1:7, Matthew 11:28–29

CONSIDER

Praising God can be quite expressive. Then again, praise often involves quietness and waiting. We sometimes forget that. Of course, quietness on the outside doesn't always mean quiet on the inside. Waiting can involve intense feelings for God. We can be almost overwhelmed with our feelings for Him. It can be hard to begin to express those feelings in words.

PONDER

* Unlike most people, God in heaven is very comfortable with silence.

* The Holy Spirit specializes in understanding our feelings beyond words.

* God's most spectacular miracles are often quiet, in the heart.

More about Praising God Isn't Always Expressive: Exodus 14:14, 1 Chronicles 16:11, Job 6:24, Psalm 141:3, Isaiah 26:3, Isaiah 30:15, Isaiah 40:31

Still more: Lamentations 3:24, Lamentations 3:26, Habakkuk 3:20, Zephaniah 3:17, 1 Thessalonians 4:11, 2 Thessalonians 3:12

Day 55

Fear of God Makes You Wiser

THE BIBLE SAYS

"He said to man, 'See, the fear of the Lord, that is wisdom. And to turn away from sin is understanding.'"

The fear of the Lord is the beginning of wisdom. All who obey His Laws have good understanding. His praise lasts forever.

The fear of the Lord is the beginning of much learning. Fools hate wisdom and teaching.

The fear of the Lord is the beginning of wisdom. To learn about the Holy One is understanding.

The fear of the Lord is the teaching for wisdom, and having no pride comes before honor.

Bible References: Job 28:28, Psalm 111:10, Proverbs 1:7, Proverbs 9:10, Proverbs 15:33

CONSIDER

Fear of God describes a growing sense of awe or reverence for who God truly is. This starts with a right understanding of who God is based on God's own Word, the Bible. As we know Him more, He imparts true wisdom to us. Everything we desire, want, and need is found in the Lord and in the Lord alone.

Anything the world, flesh, and devil offer are cheap, bitter, poisonous rip-offs designed to steal, kill, and destroy us. The wise woman turns away and looks intently at what the Bible says and becomes even more wise. She fears nothing because the Lord is the only one to whom she gives her allegiance.

PONDER

* Wisdom describes how life works best.

* Anything that contradicts God and His Word is *not* wise.

* Live with God as your King and His Word as your guide, and you will be wise.

More about Fear of God Makes You Wiser: Deuteronomy 5:29, Deuteronomy 10:12–20, Psalm 112:1, Proverbs 3:7, Ecclesiastes 12:13, Philippians 2:12

Day 56

Fear God and Trust Him

THE BIBLE SAYS

Israel saw the great power which the Lord had used against the Egyptians. And the people had fear of the Lord. They believed in the Lord and in His servant Moses.

"What does the Lord your God ask of you? He wants you to fear the Lord your God, to walk in all His ways and love Him. He wants you to serve the Lord your God with all your heart and all your soul."

"So fear the Lord. Serve Him in faith and truth."

"Only fear the Lord and be faithful to worship Him with all your heart. Think of the great things He has done for you."

We can trust God that He will do what He promised.

Bible References: Exodus 14:31, Deuteronomy 10:12, Joshua 24:14, 1 Samuel 12:24, Hebrews 10:23

CONSIDER

God wants us to fear and trust Him continually, without doubt or wavering. Yet doubt and wavering are what we often seem to do best. It's natural to doubt a stranger. . .unless he's wearing firefighter's gear and promises to take our loved one to safety.

Likewise, it's natural to doubt God. . .until we read the Bible and get to know Him. The better we get to know God, the more fully we can trust Him.

PONDER

* Those who know God best trust Him most completely—He is who He says He is.

* Those who don't know God very well struggle greatly in this life, often without hope.

* The wise woman fears God, knows Him well, and trusts Him on the deepest level.

More about Fear God and Trust Him: 1 Kings 18:21, Psalm 17:5, Psalm 26:1, Matthew 21:21, Mark 9:24, Romans 4:20–22, Jude 21

Day 57

Fear God No Matter What's Happening

THE BIBLE SAYS

We are glad for our troubles also. We know that troubles help us learn not to give up.

Everything we do shows we are God's servants. We have had to wait and suffer. We have needed things. We have been in many hard places and have had many troubles.

We are proud of you and tell the other churches about you. We tell them how your faith stays so strong even when people make it hard for you and make you suffer.

Do not throw away your trust, for your reward will be great. You must be willing to wait without giving up. After you have done what God wants you to do, God will give you what He promised you.

Remember, other Christians over all the world are suffering the same as you are. After you have suffered for awhile, God Himself will make you perfect. He will keep you in the right way. He will give you strength.

Bible References: Romans 5:3, 2 Corinthians 6:4,
2 Thessalonians 1:4, Hebrews 10:35–36, 1 Peter 5:9–10

CONSIDER

God wants us to fear and trust Him. . .no matter what.
Have you experienced abuse, grief, financial loss, pain,
or disease? No one gets through life without troubles,
but God knows, cares, and carries us through it all.

PONDER

* God designed perfection. Sin destroyed it. Troubles fill this life. But God is always for us!

* No matter what happens, we can give thanks and experience God's superlative peace.

* What troubles are you facing? Give thanks and ask the Lord for His peace today.

More about Fear God No Matter What's Happening:
2 Timothy 2:3, James 1:3, James 5:11, 1 Peter 1:5–7,
Revelation 2:10

Day 58

Fear God, Not What Might Happen

THE BIBLE SAYS

"Fear the Lord and worship Him. Listen to His voice and do not go against the Word of the Lord."

"The Lord says to you, 'Do not be afraid or troubled because of these many men. For the battle is not yours but God's.'"

"Is not your fear of God what gives you strength and your good ways that give you hope?"

The reward for not having pride and having the fear of the Lord is riches, honor and life.

"Do not fear, for I am with you. Do not be afraid, for I am your God. I will give you strength, and for sure I will help you. Yes, I will hold you up with My right hand that is right and good."

Bible References: 1 Samuel 12:14, 2 Chronicles 20:15, Job 4:6, Proverbs 22:4, Isaiah 41:10

CONSIDER

God wants us to fear and trust Him instead of fearing what might happen. To fear what might happen is to waste otherwise valuable time, energy, and resources. Most of what we worry about never happens. Or it happens far differently than what we thought or expected. True, bad things happen in this life, so be wise in what you say and do. But focus on getting to know God better so you are ready for anything.

PONDER

* To fear God is to embrace life to the full.

* To fear anything else is to dissipate and drain life.

* Ask God to give you protection, provision, and His peace.

More about Fear God, Not What Might Happen: Joshua 5:1, Nehemiah 4:14, Psalm 118:6, Isaiah 8:13, Isaiah 40:9–11, Matthew 10:28

Day 59

Fear God and Do What's Right

THE BIBLE SAYS

"For I [the Lord] have chosen [Abraham], so that he may teach his children and the sons of his house after him to keep the way of the Lord by doing what is right and fair. So the Lord may bring to Abraham what He has promised him."

"Listen well to the voice of the Lord your God. Do what is right in His eyes. Listen to what He tells you, and obey all His Laws."

"Do what is right and good in the eyes of the Lord. Then it will be well with you."

Have your roots planted deep in Christ. Grow in Him. Get your strength from Him. Let Him make you strong in the faith as you have been taught. Your life should be full of thanks to Him.

We must give thanks to God for you always, Christian brothers. It is the right thing to do because your faith is growing so much. Your love for each other is stronger all the time.

Bible References: Genesis 18:19, Exodus 15:26, Deuteronomy 6:18, Colossians 2:7, 2 Thessalonians 1:3

CONSIDER

God wants us to fear Him by continually doing what is good and right in His sight. When we see Him as the good and mighty King He is and trust Him as Lord of our lives, it is easier to obey Him.

PONDER

* Do what God says is wise. It's how life works best.

* The wise woman gladly does what is right in God's sight.

* Can you see how your life would be different if you were not listening to and obeying God?

More about Fear God and Do What's Right: Psalm 106:28–31, 2 Corinthians 1:24, Galatians 5:6, Philippians 1:25, James 2:14–17

Day 60

Do Right in God's Sight

THE BIBLE SAYS

Noah found favor in the eyes of the Lord.

"Be careful to listen to all these words I am telling you. Then it will go well with you and your children after you forever. For you will be doing what is good and right in the eyes of the Lord your God."

"Do what is right in the eyes of the Lord your God."

The eyes of the Lord are on those who do what is right and good. His ears are open to their cry.

No one can hide from God. His eyes see everything we do. We must give an answer to God for what we have done.

Bible References: Genesis 6:8, Deuteronomy 12:28, Deuteronomy 13:18, Psalm 34:15, Hebrews 4:13

CONSIDER

The world sells many competing images of what a woman's life should look and be like. Those images are built on being self-centered and living according to our own desires. Tragically, the results are guaranteed to bring disaster. Conversely, God's image is built on doing what is right in the context of a love relationship with Jesus. The results are guaranteed to bring wisdom and peace even when life doesn't seem to go our way.

PONDER

* The wise woman trusts what God sees, knows, says, and commands.

* The more a woman does what is right in God's eyes, the wiser she becomes.

* How can following God's commands actually bring more freedom and peace to your life?

More about Do Right in God's Sight: Proverbs 3:4, Proverbs 15:3, Ecclesiastes 2:26, Luke 1:15, Acts 8:21, Revelation 3:2

Still more: 1 Kings 14:8, 1 Kings 15:5, 1 Kings 22:43, 2 Kings 12:2, 2 Kings 14:3, 2 Kings 15:3, 2 Kings 15:34, 2 Kings 16:2, 2 Kings 18:3, 2 Kings 22:2, 2 Chronicles 14:2

Day 61

Live by Faith, Not by Sight

THE BIBLE SAYS

"For God's eyes are upon the ways of a man, and He sees all his steps."

The Lord's throne is in heaven. His eyes see as He tests the sons of men.

For the ways of a man are seen by the eyes of the Lord, and He watches all his paths.

"The one who is right and good will live by his faith."

Our life is lived by faith. We do not live by what we see in front of us.

Bible References: Job 34:21, Psalm 11:4, Proverbs 5:21, Habakkuk 2:4, 2 Corinthians 5:7

CONSIDER

Are you the kind of woman who has a knack for knowing what's going on in other people's lives? God doesn't just know, He understands everything going on in each of our lives. That's why we want to rely on what God sees, knows, and declares to be true. Only in heaven will we see what He sees. Until then, we trust God and live accordingly.

PONDER

* Imagine going on a trust walk at night. You're blindfolded. Your friend leads you and tells you when to turn and when to cross the street. The more you trust your friend, the easier your trust walk will be.

* Remember, you can't see what's really going on in this life let alone in the next. The more you trust God, the easier your trust walk will be.

* Open your mind to imagine the possibilities of what God may be doing in your life that you will see only in eternity.

More about Live by Faith, Not by Sight: Ezekiel 18:9, Romans 1:17, Galatians 2:20, Galatians 3:11, 2 Timothy 1:5, Hebrews 10:38

Day 62

Obey God's Commands

THE BIBLE SAYS

[Jesus:] "Teach them to do all the things I have told you. And I am with you always, even to the end of the world."

[Jesus:] "This is what I tell you to do: Love each other just as I have loved you."

We can be sure that we know Him if we obey His teaching. Anyone who says, "I know Him," but does not obey His teaching is a liar. There is no truth in him.

Loving God means to obey His Word, and His Word is not hard to obey.

Love means that we should live by obeying His Word.

Bible References: Matthew 28:20, John 15:12, 1 John 2:3-4, 1 John 5:3, 2 John 6

CONSIDER

I'm sure you figured out that "doing right" means obeying God's commands. Today's verses reveal that such obedience is much deeper than merely following rules. Our obedience comes out of loving God. We express our love for God by obeying His Word and loving each other. That's beautiful.

PONDER

* Read the Bible and affirm its truths. *Yes, I believe God always tells the truth.*

* Read the Bible and choose to obey its commands. *Yes, I read God's Word and obey it.*

* Read the Bible and choose to heed the examples given. *Yes, I read the good—and bad—examples of obeying and loving or disobeying and not loving. I choose to love and obey.*

More about Obey God's Commands: Matthew 5:19, Mark 10:19, Luke 1:6, John 15:10–11, Acts 17:30, Romans 7:12, James 1:22–25, 2 Peter 3:2, 1 John 3:22–24

Day 63

Like God, Do What's Good

THE BIBLE SAYS

Who is the man who has a desire for life, and wants to live long so that he may see good things? Keep your tongue from sin and your lips from speaking lies. . . . Do what is good. Look for peace and follow it. The eyes of the Lord are on those who do what is right and good.

Trust in the Lord, and do good.

Look for good and not sin, that you may live. Then the Lord God of All will be with you.

Remember to do good and help each other. Gifts like this please God.

The person who does what is good belongs to God.

Bible References: Psalm 34:12–15, Psalm 37:3, Amos 5:14, Hebrews 13:16, 3 John 11

CONSIDER

Do you believe in the Lord and do what is good as a demonstration of your faith? If so, you're a wise, good-hearted woman. It doesn't mean you're perfect yet. That has to wait until heaven. But you're happy to do what's good in God's eyes and do what's good for others. That can only flow from knowing and loving God.

PONDER

* God is always good. It's who He is. Every good gift is from Him.

* How can God's goodness flow out of your life today?

* Who in your life would readily say that you're a good-hearted woman?

More about Like God, Do What's Good: Isaiah 1:17, Matthew 5:16, Luke 6:27, Romans 6:4, Romans 13:12, Galatians 5:6, Galatians 6:10

Still more: Ephesians 2:10, Ephesians 4:24, 1 Thessalonians 5:15, Titus 2:14, Titus 3:8, James 1:22, 1 Peter 3:11, 1 John 2:5

Day 64

Don't Be Afraid (1 of 2)

THE BIBLE SAYS

The word of the Lord came to Abram in a special dream, saying, "Do not be afraid, Abram. I am your safe place. Your reward will be very great."

Then the angel of God called to Hagar from heaven, and said, "Why are you so troubled, Hagar? Do not be afraid. For God has heard the cry of the boy."

The Lord showed Himself to Isaac that same night, and said, "I am the God of your father Abraham. Do not be afraid, for I am with you. I will bring good to you."

Moses said to the people, "Do not be afraid! Be strong, and see how the Lord will save you today. For the Egyptians you have seen today, you will never see again."

"The Lord is the One Who goes before you. He will be with you. He will be faithful to you and will not leave you alone. Do not be afraid or troubled."

Bible References: Genesis 15:1, Genesis 21:17, Genesis 26:24, Exodus 14:13, Deuteronomy 31:8

CONSIDER

Contrary to popular belief, "Fear not" and related phrases don't appear in the Bible 365 times. Depending on the translation, the Bible says "Fear not" some 95 to 115 times. That should be sufficient! Then again, how often does the Bible have to say something for it to be true?

PONDER

✳ Why does God have to say, "Fear not"?

✳ Why do angels have to say, "Fear not"?

✳ What does it take for you to "fear not"?

More about Don't Be Afraid: Joshua 1:9, Joshua 10:8, 1 Samuel 12:20, 2 Kings 6:16, 1 Chronicles 22:13, 2 Chronicles 20:15–17, 2 Chronicles 32:7, Isaiah 41:10–13

Day 65

Don't Be Afraid (2 of 2)

THE BIBLE SAYS

[Jesus:] "I say to you, My friends, do not be afraid of those who kill the body and then can do no more."

[Jesus:] "Peace I leave with you. My peace I give to you. I do not give peace to you as the world gives. Do not let your hearts be troubled or afraid."

Paul saw the Lord in a dream one night. He said to Paul, "Do not be afraid. Keep speaking. Do not close your mouth."

Pray for me also. Pray that I might open my mouth without fear. . . . I want to keep on speaking for Christ without fear the way I should.

God has said, "I will never leave you or let you be alone." So we can say for sure, "The Lord is my Helper. I am not afraid of anything man can do to me."

Bible References: Luke 12:4, John 14:27, Acts 18:9, Ephesians 6:19–20, Hebrews 13:5–6

CONSIDER

Fear, and the circumstances around it, produce fight, flight, or freeze responses. Wise women, however, learn a fourth response to fear: focus. That is, focus on God (who He is) and His Word (what He says to be true). That, by far, is the smartest, strongest response.

PONDER

* How quickly can you replace fear with focus?

* Choose a truth about God on which to focus.

* Choose a Bible verse to memorize and recite especially when you feel afraid.

More about Don't Be Afraid: Matthew 8:26, Matthew 10:26, Matthew 14:27, Matthew 28:10, Mark 6:50, Luke 5:10, Luke 12:7, Luke 12:32, John 6:20, Acts 9:27, 1 Peter 3:14, 1 John 4:18

Day 66

Be Strong and Courageous (1 of 2)

THE BIBLE SAYS

Then the Lord said to Joshua the son of Nun, "Be strong and have strength of heart. For you will bring the people of Israel into the land I promised them. And I will be with you."

"Only be strong and have much strength of heart. Be careful to obey all the Law which My servant Moses told you. Do not turn from it to the right or to the left. Then all will go well with you everywhere you go."

Then Joshua said to them, "Do not be afraid or troubled. Be strong and have strength of heart. For the Lord will do this to all who hate you and fight against you."

When Saul saw any strong man, or any man with strength of heart, he would have the man join him.

"I have seen a son of Jesse the Bethlehemite who plays music well. He is a man with strength of heart, a man of war, wise in his speaking, and good-looking. And the Lord is with him."

Bible References: Deuteronomy 31:23, Joshua 1:7, Joshua 10:25, 1 Samuel 14:52, 1 Samuel 16:18

CONSIDER

Be strong. Have strength of heart. Be courageous. Which women do you know who exhibit these traits in abundance? Perhaps a widow or cancer survivor or mother of special-needs children. Being strong and courageous has nothing to do with personality or talent and everything to do with trusting God's presence.

PONDER

* What makes a woman "strong"?

* How do strength and courage come from the Lord?

* What does it take to be a strong and courageous woman?

More about Be Strong and Courageous: 1 Chronicles 22:13, 1 Chronicles 28:20, 2 Chronicles 16:9, 2 Chronicles 32:7, Psalm 27:14

Day 67

Be Strong and Courageous (2 of 2)

THE BIBLE SAYS

At once Jesus spoke to them and said, "Take hope. It is I. Do not be afraid!"

[Jesus:] "I have told you these things so you may have peace in Me. In the world you will have much trouble. But take hope! I have power over the world!"

Our hope comes from God. May He fill you with joy and peace because of your trust in Him. May your hope grow stronger by the power of the Holy Spirit.

Watch and keep awake! Stand true to the Lord. Keep on acting like men and be strong.

This is the last thing I want to say: Be strong with the Lord's strength.

Bible References: Matthew 14:27, John 16:33, Romans 15:13, 1 Corinthians 16:13, Ephesians 6:10

CONSIDER

The cowardly disciples in the four Gospels become

bold, courageous, and daring individuals in the book of Acts. What happened? God's Word came alive when they saw it fulfilled. They spent six weeks with the resurrected Lord Jesus. A few days later, the Holy Spirit filled their hearts and lives. From then on, they were convinced that laying down their lives for the Lord was a privilege to spread the Gospel across the known world.

PONDER

* Time in God's Word? Yes, you're doing that daily reading *The 3-Minute Bible Habit for Women*.

* Trust in the resurrected Lord Jesus? Yes, you have embraced the Good News as your own.

* Filled by the Holy Spirit? Yes, you have confessed any sin and want to live boldly for God.

More about Be Strong and Courageous: Mark 6:50, Luke 2:40, Acts 4:13, 1 Corinthians 15:58, 2 Timothy 1:7, 1 Peter 5:10, 1 John 5:5

Day 68

Love and Obey God, Be Blessed (1 of 2)

THE BIBLE SAYS

"Now then, if you will obey My voice and keep My agreement, you will belong to Me from among all nations. For all the earth is Mine."

"I show loving-kindness to thousands of those who love Me and keep My Laws."

"So keep My Laws and do what I say. If a man obeys them, My Laws will be life for him. I am the Lord."

Who is the man who fears the Lord? He will teach him in the way he should choose.

Happy is the man You choose and bring near to You to live in Your holy place. We will be filled with the good things of Your house, Your holy house.

Bible References: Exodus 19:5, Exodus 20:6, Leviticus 18:5, Psalm 25:12, Psalm 65:4

CONSIDER

We know that God doesn't promise an easy, trouble-free life, but can we see that God offers us a *good* life? Such a life is the opposite of what the world offers. It's quiet, Christ-centered, faithful, without fanfare. It's a life rooted deeply in loving God and loving others. This life is lived with eternity always in view; it is not focused on temporary pleasures and perks. God's gift of a "happy life" looks different but satisfies more.

PONDER

* Why does God love us so much?

* Why does God want us to enjoy happy and blessed lives?

* What do you choose to embrace to enjoy such a life?

More about Love and Obey God, Be Blessed: Genesis 48:15–16, Exodus 23:13, Deuteronomy 30:19–20, Joshua 24:15, Proverbs 22:6, Isaiah 56:4–5

Day 69

Love and Obey God, Be Blessed (2 of 2)

THE BIBLE SAYS

[Jesus:] "The person who is not ashamed of Me and does not turn away from Me is happy."

Jesus said to him, "Thomas, because you have seen Me, you believe. Those are happy who have never seen Me and yet believe!"

Do not let yourselves get tired of doing good. If we do not give up, we will get what is coming to us at the right time.

The man who does not give up when tests come is happy. After the test is over, he will receive the crown of life. God has promised this to those who love Him.

Watch yourselves! You do not want to lose what we have worked for. You want to get what has been promised to you.

Bible References: Luke 7:23, John 20:29, Galatians 6:9, James 1:12, 2 John 8

CONSIDER

Being blessed isn't a one time experience. A blessed life comes from keeping on keeping on: trusting Jesus, doing what is right, believing God's rewards are coming. Being blessed can be thrown away when we give up our trust, stop obeying, give in to the temptations of pride, lust, greed, or fear. Instead, keep loving and obeying each day your whole life long.

PONDER

* For you, is the blessed life a current or past or perhaps future experience?

* What is the result and reward of not giving up on trusting and obeying God?

* Why do so many women (and men) give up and lose out later in their lives?

More about Love and Obey God, Be Blessed: Matthew 5:3-11, Matthew 11:6, Luke 6:20-23, Romans 6:16-19, Ephesians 1:3, Revelation 1:3, Revelation 22:7

Day 70

Praise God and Honor Others

THE BIBLE SAYS

"Honor your father and your mother, so your life may be long in the land the Lord your God gives you."

"Show respect to the person with white hair. Honor an older person and you will honor your God. I am the Lord. If a stranger lives with you in your land, do not do wrong to him. You should act toward the stranger who lives among you as you would toward one born among you. Love him as you love yourself."

"Proud," "Self-important" and "One who laughs at the truth" are the names of the man who acts without respect and is proud.

Be willing to help and care for each other because of Christ. By doing this, you honor Christ.

Show respect to all men. Love the Christians. Honor God with love and fear. Respect the head leader of the country.

Bible References: Exodus 20:12, Leviticus 19:32–34, Proverbs 21:24, Ephesians 5:21, 1 Peter 2:17

CONSIDER

God wants us to praise Him and also give honor to others. God's Word says eight times, "Honor your father and your mother." The Bible also says to honor church leaders who serve well. Scripture even says to honor government officials, including the emperor, and pray for them. We live in a day and age that dishonors. Whom can you honor today?

PONDER

* Why does dishonoring others come so easily?

* Why does honoring others come so slowly?

* Whom will you choose to honor today?

More about Praise God and Honor Others: Leviticus 19:3, Romans 13:7, Philippians 2:29, 1 Timothy 2:1–4, 1 Timothy 5:17, Hebrews 13:17

Day 71

The Joy of a Pure Heart

THE BIBLE SAYS

Let the sins of the sinful stop. But build up those who are right with You. For the God Who is right and good tests both the hearts and the minds. I am kept safe by God, Who saves those who are pure in heart.

Sing for joy in the Lord, you who are right with Him. It is right for the pure in heart to praise Him.

Keep on giving Your loving-kindness to those who know You. Keep on being right and good to the pure in heart.

[Jesus:] "Those who have a pure heart are happy, because they will see God."

You have made your souls pure by obeying the truth through the Holy Spirit. This has given you a true love for the Christians. Let it be a true love from the heart.

Bible References: Psalm 7:9–10, Psalm 33:1, Psalm 36:10, Matthew 5:8, 1 Peter 1:22

CONSIDER

Maybe you don't see yourself as a "pure-hearted" woman. Who uses that language these days? What woman can say she doesn't have envious or critical thoughts and desires? You're not pure-hearted because you're perfect. You're pure-hearted when your deepest heart longing is to love and obey God.

PONDER

* Is anything keeping you from a pure heart? If so. . .

* Confess your sins and ask the Lord to forgive you. Then. . .

* Ask for the Holy Spirit to fill every fiber of your being once again.

More about The Joy of a Pure Heart: 1 Kings 3:6, Psalm 24:4, Psalm 73:1, Psalm 97:11, Proverbs 4:23, 1 Timothy 1:5

Day 72

Who Is Happy and Blessed

THE BIBLE SAYS

It is You Who saves, O Lord. May You bring happiness to Your people.

Let those who are right and good be glad. Let them be happy before God. Yes, let them be full of joy.

How happy are the people who know the sound of joy! They walk in the light of Your face, O Lord.

Day after day they went to the house of God together. In their houses they ate their food together. Their hearts were happy.

I have learned the secret of being happy at all times.

Bible References: Psalm 3:8, Psalm 68:3, Psalm 89:15, Acts 2:46, Philippians 4:12

CONSIDER

God is infinitely and eternally happy and blessed. It is who He is. It's no surprise, then, that God wants to bring joy and happiness to His people. It doesn't mean we don't feel other emotions or experience pain. But when we love God and do what is right in His sight, we experience deep measures of happiness and blessings. That happiness is multiplied when we share our lives with other joy-filled Christians who know and love God as well.

PONDER

* Why is God always happy and blessed?

* Why are times with other joy-filled Christians important?

* Who is the most joy-filled Christian you know? Why is he or she like that?

More about Who Is Happy and Blessed: 1 Samuel 2:1, Psalm 1:1, Psalm 16:11, Psalm 17:15, Psalm 32:1, Psalm 37:4, Psalm 41:1, Psalm 84:12, Psalm 106:3, Psalm 119:162, Psalm 128:1, Proverbs 3:13

Still more: John 20:29, Acts 20:35, Romans 12:12, 2 Corinthians 12:9, Ephesians 6:7, 1 Thessalonians 2:9, 1 Timothy 6:17

Day 73

God Gives Good Gifts in Abundance

THE BIBLE SAYS

They are filled with the riches of Your house. And You give them a drink from Your river of joy.

You brought us out into a place where we have much more than we need.

"Test Me in this [tithing]," says the Lord of All. "See if I will not then open the windows of heaven and pour out good things for you until there is no more need."

[Jesus:] "I came so they might have life, a great full life."

Let us honor and thank the God and Father of our Lord Jesus Christ. He has already given us a taste of what heaven is like.

Bible References: Psalm 36:8, Psalm 66:12, Malachi 3:10, John 10:10, Ephesians 1:3

CONSIDER

God blessed many Old Testament believers with great wealth. As well, God promised to give good gifts to all His Jewish people if they obeyed His commands. The Lord strongly desires to give good gifts to us even today. Not the great wealth He gave to Old Testament believers but everything we need to live good and loving lives. God also gives generously to those who love to give generously to others.

PONDER

* Why is God so intent on giving good gifts to us?

* Take a moment to thank the Lord for spiritual blessings.

* Take a moment to thank the Lord for something "simple" or "ordinary" in your life. God delights to see you enjoy all His good and perfect gifts!

More about God Gives Good Gifts in Abundance: Deuteronomy 8:9, Deuteronomy 28:8, Deuteronomy 28:11, Deuteronomy 30:9, Deuteronomy 33:15

Still more: Nehemiah 9:25, Proverbs 10:22, John 16:24, Romans 5:20, Ephesians 1:4–18

Day 74

Jesus Christ's Promises to the Generous

THE BIBLE SAYS

Jesus looked at him with love and said, "There is one thing for you to do yet. Go and sell everything you have and give the money to poor people. You will have riches in heaven. Then come and follow Me."

[Jesus:] "Sell what you have and give the money to poor people. Have money-bags for yourselves that will never wear out. These money-bags are riches in heaven that will always be there."

[Jesus:] "When you have a supper, ask poor people. Ask those who cannot walk and those who are blind."

Zaccheus stood up and said to the Lord, "Lord, see! Half of what I own I will give to poor people. And if I have taken money from anyone in a wrong way, I will pay him back four times as much."

Give something to poor people.

Bible References: Mark 10:21, Luke 12:33, Luke 14:13, Luke 19:8, John 13:29

CONSIDER

Jesus and His followers gave generously and sacrificially to the destitute and distressed. As you and I grow in wisdom and wealth, we can give even more sacrificially. Perhaps it's sponsoring a child overseas or helping rescue a relative from homelessness. God loves and blesses women who love to give like He does.

PONDER

* Jesus had a special love for the poor, distressed, wounded, and homeless.

* Jesus wanted His followers to show great love to them as well.

* Who needs your generosity to rescue them this year?

More about Jesus Christ's Promises to the Generous: Matthew 19:21, Matthew 25:31–40, Matthew 26:9, Mark 14:5, Luke 11:41, Luke 18:22

Still more: Acts 9:36, Acts 10:2, Acts 10:4, Acts 10:31, Acts 24:17

Day 75

Rest in God's Peace and Abundant Provisions

THE BIBLE SAYS

And the land had peace for forty years.

Midian was put under the power of the people of Israel. They did not lift up their heads any more. And the land had peace for forty years, during the life of Gideon.

"See, a son will be born to you, who will be a man of peace. I will give him peace from all those who hate him on every side. His name will be Solomon."

The nation of Jehoshaphat was at peace. His God gave him rest on all sides.

Then my people will live in a place of peace, in safe homes, and in quiet resting places.

Bible References: Judges 5:31, Judges 8:28, 1 Chronicles 22:9, 2 Chronicles 20:30, Isaiah 32:18

CONSIDER

In the Old Writings, God's good gifts were enjoyed by leaders and God's people both in the absence of war (peace) and in the abundance of provisions (no need). This peace and provision came when the people obeyed. Sadly, these times of peace were rarer than times of war. Peace is not a human invention, nor is peace the norm. Someday, God will bring true and complete peace to the world.

PONDER

* Do you consider yourself to have lived in times of peace or war?

* How have you experienced God's peace and prosperity up until now?

* Thank God for peace, and look forward to true peace when God's kingdom finally comes in full.

More about Rest in God's Peace and Abundant Provisions: Judges 3:1, Judges 3:30, 2 Kings 20:19, 2 Chronicles 14:1-7, Psalm 147:14, Proverbs 3:2, Isaiah 39:8, 1 Timothy 2:2

Day 76

Make Others Happy with God's Peace

THE BIBLE SAYS

[Mordecai] worked for the good of his people and spoke for the well-being of all the Jews.

[Jesus:] "Those who make peace are happy, because they will be called the sons of God."

Jesus said to her, "Daughter, your faith has healed you. Go in peace."

[Jesus:] "When you go into a house, say that you hope peace will come to them. If a man who loves peace lives there, your good wishes will come to him."

Work for the things that make peace and help each other become stronger Christians.

Bible References: Esther 10:3, Matthew 5:9, Luke 8:48, Luke 10:5–6, Romans 14:19

CONSIDER

Both in the Bible and now, Jewish people greet each other by saying, "Shalom." They are wishing health, peace, protection, provision, and prosperity to one another. They are saying, "May you be full of well-being." That's the kind of peace that God gives to those who love Him and that we can give to one another.

PONDER

* Have you ever "received" peace from another person? What did they say? How did you respond?

* In what ways would a woman be able to "go in peace" after being healed or forgiven by Jesus?

* To whom can you "give" peace today? What will you say? And how do you think they will respond?

More about Make Others Happy with God's Peace:
Matthew 10:11–13, Mark 5:34, Luke 7:50, John 14:27, John 20:21, Acts 15:33, Acts 16:36, Romans 12:18, James 2:16, James 3:18

Day 77

Bring Happiness to One Another

THE BIBLE SAYS

[Jesus:] "You are to love each other. You must love each other as I have loved you. If you love each other, all men will know you are My followers."

Love each other as Christian brothers. Show respect for each other.

Receive each other as Christ received you. This will honor God.

Work to get along with others. Live in peace. The God of love and peace will be with you.

You must be kind to each other. Think of the other person. Forgive other people just as God forgave you because of Christ's death on the cross.

Bible References: John 13:34–35, Romans 12:10, Romans 15:7, 2 Corinthians 13:11, Ephesians 4:32

CONSIDER

The Bible says we bless one another by our love. That

love is expressed when we spend time together and share with each other. Sometimes we give gifts in secret; sometimes we give to others openly by including the extra gift of our presence. Just the right gift brings happiness to the one who receives it—especially the gifts of kindness, respect, forgiveness, and peace.

PONDER

- ✳ Do you know your love language—what makes you feel loved and how you express your love?

- ✳ How are love and happiness connected? How else are they connected?

- ✳ Love. Honor. Respect. Harmony. Kindness. Thoughtfulness. Forgiveness. Listening to someone's whole story. Expressing gratitude. Offering a winsome smile. What intangible gifts can you give to someone today?

More about Bring Happiness to One Another: Romans 12:16, Galatians 5:13, Ephesians 4:2, Colossians 3:1, Hebrews 3:1, Hebrews 10:25, 1 Peter 3:8

Day 78

Never Praise the Rich and Famous

THE BIBLE SAYS

The Lord says, "On that day I will destroy the wise men from Edom and understanding from Mount Esau."

Be sure of this! No person who does sex sins or who is not pure will have any part in the holy nation of Christ and of God. The same is true for the person who always wants what other people have. This becomes a god to him.

Destroy the desires to sin that are in you. These desires are: sex sins, anything that is not clean, a desire for sex sins, and wanting something someone else has. This is worshiping a god.

In the past you gave enough of your life over to living like the people who do not know God.

No one who is sinful-minded or tells lies can go in. Only those whose names are written in the Lamb's book of life can go in.

Bible References: Obadiah 8, Ephesians 5:5, Colossians 3:5, 1 Peter 4:3, Revelation 21:27

CONSIDER

Our culture worships the rich and famous—even when they live greedy or sexually corrupt lives. Scripture couldn't be more clear-cut that our praise should go only and always to the one true God. It never goes to anyone else, no matter how ultra-smart, ultra-powerful, and ultra-beautiful they may seem to be.

PONDER

* Why do the world, the flesh, and the devil promote celebrities?

* Why is it easy to adore, follow, and imitate certain celebrities?

* Which celebrities do you need out of your life immediately?

More about Never Praise the Rich and Famous: Exodus 20:3–5, Leviticus 26:1, Jeremiah 25:6, Acts 17:16, Romans 1:23, 1 Corinthians 5:11, 1 Corinthians 6:9–10, 1 Corinthians 10:14

Day 79

Why God Sometimes Disciplines Us

THE BIBLE SAYS

"Know in your heart that the Lord your God was punishing you just as a man punishes his son."

My son, listen when the Lord punishes you. Do not give up when He tells you what you must do. The Lord punishes everyone He loves.

Do you remember what God said to you when He called you His sons? "My son, listen when the Lord punishes you. Do not give up when He tells you what you must do. The Lord punishes everyone He loves."

Do not give up when you are punished by God. Be willing to take it, knowing that God is teaching you as a son. Is there a father who does not punish his son sometimes?

[Jesus:] "I speak strong words to those I love and I punish them. Have a strong desire to please the Lord. Be sorry for your sins and turn from them."

Bible References: Deuteronomy 8:5, Proverbs 3:11–12, Hebrews 12:5–6, Hebrews 12:7, Revelation 3:19

CONSIDER

The Bible verses above use the word *punish*, but God means something very different than what we may have experienced as children. First, God corrects us in love. Second, God disciplines us for our own good. Third, God cultivates happy obedience to Him.

PONDER

* Remember the world, the flesh, and the devil? They pull you away from God's Word, wisdom, and ways.

* Remember Jesus Christ? He was sinless, yet He willingly endured shame, humiliation, beatings, torture, crucifixion, and death.

* Remember the Holy Spirit? He rejoices when you accept God's discipline.

More about Why God Sometimes Disciplines Us: Psalm 94:12, Isaiah 38:16, 1 Corinthians 11:32, 2 Timothy 1:7, Titus 1:8, Hebrews 12:8–11

Day 80

Weep Over Those Who
Keep Saying No

THE BIBLE SAYS

My heart cries out for Moab.

I will cry with much sorrow for Jazer and for the vines of Sibmah.

I said, "Turn your eyes away from me. Let me cry with much sorrow. Do not try to comfort me about my people being destroyed."

If only my head were a well of water, and my eyes a well of tears, that I might cry day and night for my people who have been killed!

When Jesus came near the city, He cried as He saw it. He said, "If you had only known on this great day the things that make peace! But now they are hidden from your eyes."

Bible References: Isaiah 15:5, Isaiah 16:9, Isaiah 22:4, Jeremiah 9:1, Luke 19:41–42

CONSIDER

Jesus and the early preachers wept ahead of time over those who always said no to God before their deaths. Scripture clearly and consistently teaches that God doesn't want anyone to die in their sins and live eternally apart from Him. Instead, the Lord wants everyone to turn from their sins and turn instead to Him. He offers them forgiveness, salvation, eternal life, and so much more. Millions continue to say no, but God never stops wooing their hearts.

PONDER

* Why would anyone persistently say no to God?

* Do you know anyone who turned to God shortly before dying? Thank God for His mercy.

* Pray for any loved one who continues to say no to God. Cry out for God's mercy.

More about Weep Over Those Who Keep Saying No: Job 35:12, Jeremiah 9:10, Jeremiah 13:17, Lamentations 1:16, Lamentations 2:11, Matthew 23:37, Luke 13:34–35, 2 Peter 3:9, Revelation 1:7

Day 81

Do Your Work Quietly and Well

THE BIBLE SAYS

This man is like a tree planted by rivers of water, which gives its fruit at the right time and its leaf never dries up. Whatever he does will work out well for him.

Trust your work to the Lord, and your plans will work out well.

The work of being right and good will give peace. From the right and good work will come quiet trust forever. Then my people will live in a place of peace, in safe homes, and in quiet resting places.

"Work for the well-being of the city where I have sent you to and pray to the Lord for this. For if it is well with the city you live in, it will be well with you."

Do your best to live a quiet life. Learn to do your own work well. We told you about this before.

Bible References: Psalm 1:3, Proverbs 16:3, Isaiah 32:17–18, Jeremiah 29:7, 1 Thessalonians 4:11

CONSIDER

A new weed is portable. If you wish, you can transplant it every day. A well-established fruit tree is fixed in the ground. If you want to enjoy its fruit, leave it where it is. The deeper the roots, the more delicious fruit it will bear year after year. Your life in Jesus Christ is like that—as you keep on keeping on in the Christian faith, your life bears more and better fruit, and God uses that fruit to bless others.

PONDER

* What's wrong with weeds?

* What's right with fruit trees?

* Do you want to grow deeper?

More about Do Your Work Quietly and Well: 2 Chronicles 31:21, 1 Corinthians 15:58, 1 Timothy 2:1–4, 2 Timothy 3:17, James 4:10

Day 82

After Death, Rest in Peace

THE BIBLE SAYS

"You will live many years, die in peace and be buried."

"For now I would have lain down and been quiet. I would have slept then. I would have been at rest."

"The man who is right with God is taken away from what is sinful, and goes where there is peace."

Joseph took the body of Jesus down from the cross. He put the linen cloth he had bought around the body. Then he laid the body in a grave which had been cut out in the side of a rock.

Everything in heaven and on earth can come to God because of Christ's death on the cross. Christ's blood has made peace.

Bible References: Genesis 15:15, Job 3:13, Isaiah 57:1–2, Mark 15:46, Colossians 1:20

CONSIDER

People say, "Rest in peace," to talk about relief from life's pain. Jesus gives true peace now. . .and after death. Jesus is the embodiment of God's rest and peace for you and me. We sometimes forget the Good News includes the fact that Jesus was buried and laid to rest in a grave. But the peace came when He rose again and ascended to heaven. Our peace will be real when we are with Him in heaven too!

PONDER

* When you think about dying, are you filled with peace?

* If yes, what fills you with such peace?

* If no, what prevents you from experiencing such peace?

More about After Death, Rest in Peace: Isaiah 53:5, Matthew 27:60, Luke 19:42, Luke 23:53, John 19:41–42, Acts 10:36, Acts 13:29

Day 83

With God in Heaven Someday

THE BIBLE SAYS

"I will make new heavens and a new earth. The past things will not be remembered or come to mind."

"For the Lord of All says, 'Once again, in a little while, I am going to shake the heavens and the earth, the sea and the dry land.'"

[Jesus:] "There are many rooms in My Father's house. If it were not so, I would have told you. I am going away to make a place for you. After I go and make a place for you, I will come back and take you with Me. Then you may be where I am."

Our body is like a house we live in here on earth. When it is destroyed, we know that God has another body for us in heaven.

We are looking for what God has promised, which are new heavens and a new earth. Only what is right and good will be there.

Bible References: Isaiah 65:17, Haggai 2:6, John 14:2-3, 2 Corinthians 5:1, 2 Peter 3:13

CONSIDER

We talk about being in heaven with God after we die—
if we belong to Jesus! But one day God also will
make a brand-new, better-than-ever universe. Each
of us will receive a new body and spend eternity with
God in those new heavens and that new earth.

PONDER

* Take a moment and imagine living with God, without sin and without pain. Smile and thank Him!
  Or shout and dance. The news is just that good!

* What would you do without the limits of a sinful
  and mortal body? Someday, you will!

* Remember, God has more in store for the rest
  of eternity!

---

*More about With God in Heaven Someday: Isaiah 66:22,
1 Corinthians 15:35–58, Hebrews 12:26–27, Revelation
20:11, Revelation 21:1*

*Still more: Genesis 3:17–19, Isaiah 24:5–6, Jeremiah
12:4, Hosea 4:3, Romans 8:19*

Day 84

Jesus Christ Is Seated in Heaven

THE BIBLE SAYS

The Lord says to my Lord, "Sit at My right side, for those who hate You will be a place to rest Your feet."

[Jesus:] "When the Son of Man comes in His shining-greatness, He will sit down on His throne of greatness. All the angels will be with Him."

After Jesus had talked to them, He was taken up into heaven. He sat down on the right side of God.

It is the same power that raised Christ from the dead. This same power put Christ at God's right side in heaven.

The Son gave His own life so we could be clean from all sin. After He had done that, He sat down on the right side of God in heaven.

Bible References: Psalm 110:1, Matthew 25:31, Mark 16:19, Ephesians 1:20, Hebrews 1:3

CONSIDER

We don't have to wonder where Jesus Christ is. The Bible makes it clear that He is seated on a great throne with honor at God the Father's right hand. The Father and Son love to be together. The Father has put everything under Jesus Christ's rule, dominion, and authority. Jesus truly is the King of kings and Lord of lords. The Father couldn't be happier.

PONDER

* Jesus was seated with honor next to the Father for all eternity.

* It's from His place beside the Father that Jesus prays for us today.

* How does considering Jesus on His throne change your perspective?

More about Jesus Christ Is Seated in Heaven: Matthew 19:28, Matthew 22:44, Mark 12:36, Luke 20:42, Acts 2:33–34, Acts 5:31, Acts 7:55–56, Romans 8:34, Hebrews 8:1, Hebrews 10:12

Day 85

Jesus Christ's Shining-Greatness Forever

THE BIBLE SAYS

[Jesus:] "Then something special will be seen in the sky telling of the Son of Man. All nations of the earth will have sorrow. They will see the Son of Man coming in the clouds of the sky with power and shining-greatness."

So when the name of Jesus is spoken, everyone in heaven and on earth and under the earth will bow down before Him. And every tongue will say Jesus Christ is Lord. Everyone will give honor to God the Father.

When He received honor and shining-greatness from God the Father, a voice came to Him from the All-powerful God, saying, "This is My much-loved Son. I am very happy with Him."

Grow in the loving-favor that Christ gives you. Learn to know our Lord Jesus Christ better. He is the One Who saves. May He have all the shining-greatness now and forever. Let it be so.

"The Lamb Who was killed has the right to receive

power and riches and wisdom and strength and honor and shining-greatness and thanks."

Bible References: Matthew 24:30, Philippians 2:10–11, 2 Peter 1:17, 2 Peter 3:18, Revelation 5:12

CONSIDER

Jesus deserves all honor, shining-greatness, and praise forever. One day He will return with great power and shining-greatness. Everyone will bow their knee and confess Jesus is Lord. This will bring great honor to the Father.

PONDER

* The Father, Son, and Spirit share shining-greatness forever.
* The Father wants everyone to worship His Son, Jesus Christ.
* Why do some people resist worshipping Jesus?

More about Jesus Christ's Shining-Greatness Forever: Matthew 16:27, Matthew 24:64, John 5:23, Acts 1:11, 2 Thessalonians 1:7–8, 2 Thessalonians 1:12, 1 Timothy 6:15–16, Hebrews 1:6, Revelation 22:12

Day 86

Jesus Christ Is Coming Again

THE BIBLE SAYS

[Jesus:] "The Son of Man will come in the greatness of His Father with His angels. Then He will give to every man his pay as he has worked."

[Jesus:] "When the Son of Man comes in His shining-greatness, He will sit down on His throne of greatness. All the angels will be with Him."

[Jesus:] "Whoever is ashamed of Me and My Words among the sinful people of this day, the Son of Man will be ashamed of him when He comes in the shining-greatness of His Father and His holy angels."

We are to be looking for the great hope and the coming of our great God and the One Who saves, Christ Jesus.

The day of the Lord will come as a robber comes.

Bible References: Matthew 16:27, Matthew 25:31, Mark 8:38, Titus 2:13, 2 Peter 3:10

CONSIDER

Many people scoff at the idea that Jesus Christ is coming again. This idea, however, is more than a literary hint or clue. It's woven throughout the Bible, appearing hundreds of times in the New Testament alone. Jesus Himself said it clearly: He's coming again! Look and long for Him today.

PONDER

* What will Jesus Christ's second coming mean for those who reject Him?

* What will Christ's return mean for those who know and love Him?

* Do you think it is possible that Jesus will return in your lifetime?

More about Jesus Christ Is Coming Again: Matthew 24:30, John 14:1–3, Acts 1:11, 1 Thessalonians 4:14, 2 Thessalonians 1:7–8, 2 Timothy 4:1, Hebrews 9:28, 2 Peter 1:19, Revelation 19:11

Day 87

Jesus Is the First and Last

THE BIBLE SAYS

[Jesus:] "I am the First and the Last."

He laid His right hand on me and said, "Do not be afraid. I am the First and the Last."

[Jesus:] "The One Who is First and Last, the One Who died and came to life again, says this: I know of your troubles."

Then the One sitting on the throne said, "See! I am making all things new. Write, for these words are true and faithful." Then He said to me, "These things have happened! I am the First and the Last. I am the beginning and the end. To anyone who is thirsty, I will give the water of life. It is a free gift."

[Jesus:] "See! I am coming soon. I am bringing with Me the reward I will give to everyone for what he has done. I am the First and the Last. I am the beginning and the end."

Bible References: Revelation 1:11, Revelation1:17, Revelation 22:12-13, Revelation 21:5-6, Revelation 22:12-13

CONSIDER

Only the one true God is eternal—that is, always existent from eternity past to eternity future. This is especially clear in the Old Writings by the early preacher Isaiah. Yet Jesus Christ repeatedly describes Himself in the same ways. He was in the beginning, before creation. He is the final climax in eternity to come. Jesus is all in all!

PONDER

* What is true of God is infinitely and eternally true of God.

* What is true of the Father is true of the Son and Spirit.

* We have no reason to hesitate worshipping Jesus.

More about Jesus Is the First and Last: Isaiah 41:4, Isaiah 43:10, Isaiah 48:12, Revelation 1:8

Day 88

We Will Feast Together in Heaven

THE BIBLE SAYS

On this mountain the Lord of All will make a supper of good things ready for all people. It will be a supper of good wine, of the best foods, and of fine wine.

[Jesus:] "I say to you, many people will come from the east and from the west. They will sit down with Abraham and with Isaac and with Jacob in the holy nation of heaven."

Again Jesus spoke to them in picture-stories. He said, "The holy nation of heaven is like a king who gave a wedding supper for his son."

"Let us be full of joy and be glad. Let us honor Him, for the time has come for the wedding supper of the Lamb. His bride has made herself ready."

The angel said to me, "Write this: 'Those who are asked to the wedding supper of the Lamb are happy.'" And he said, "These are the true words of God."

Bible References: Isaiah 25:6, Matthew 8:11, Matthew 22:1–2, Revelation 19:7, Revelation 19:9

CONSIDER

Do you like going to large celebratory dinners? Jesus did! He enjoyed the opportunity to meet new people and whet their appetites for heaven. In His preaching and teaching, Jesus spoke of the wonderful supper in heaven and how great it will be for those who accept His invitation. When we gather together with Him, the celebration won't stop and will never grow dull!

PONDER

* What is the most enjoyable celebration you have attended?

* What did you enjoy most about that celebration?

* We will have the time of our lives celebrating with Jesus someday!

More about We Will Feast Together in Heaven: Luke 13:29, Luke 14:15, Luke 22:15–16, Luke 22:17–18, Luke 22:29–30

Day 89

We Can Receive Crowns in Heaven

THE BIBLE SAYS

My eyes are on the crown. I want to win the race and get the crown of God's call from heaven through Christ Jesus.

There is a crown which comes from being right with God. The Lord, the One Who will judge, will give it to me on that great day when He comes again. I will not be the only one to receive a crown. All those who love to think of His coming and are looking for Him will receive one also.

The man who does not give up when tests come is happy. After the test is over, he will receive the crown of life. God has promised this to those who love Him.

When the Head Shepherd comes again, you [church leaders] will get the crown of shining-greatness that will not come to an end.

[Jesus:]"Be faithful even to death. Then I will give you the crown of life."

Bible References: Philippians 3:14, 2 Timothy 4:8, James 1:12, 1 Peter 5:4, Revelation 2:10

CONSIDER

We sometimes forget that wedding rings aren't always just single rings. We also sometimes forget that royalty doesn't own and wear just one single crown. Sometimes they own a collection of gorgeous and super expensive crowns, diadems, and tiaras. True, we may give all our crowns back to the Lord Jesus. Still, let's win as many as we can!

PONDER

* What is the point of a royal crown here on earth?

* What is the point of earning crowns from the Lord?

* Look at the verses again. Do you see which crowns you will be given when you are with God?

More about We Can Receive Crowns in Heaven: Psalm 21:3, 1 Corinthians 9:24, Colossians 2:18, 2 Timothy 2:5, Revelation 3:11

Day 90

We Can Look Forward to Rich Rewards

THE BIBLE SAYS

[Jesus:] "Be glad and full of joy because your reward will be much in heaven."

The one who plants and the one who waters are alike. Each one will receive his own reward.

Whatever work you do, do it with all your heart. Do it for the Lord and not for men. Remember that you will get your reward from the Lord. He will give you what you should receive.

The truth is in us and will be with us forever. Loving-favor and loving-kindness and peace are ours as we live in truth and love. These come from God the Father and from the Lord Jesus Christ, Who is the Son of the Father.

[Jesus:] "See! I am coming soon. I am bringing with Me the reward I will give to everyone for what he has done."

Bible References: Matthew 5:12, 1 Corinthians 3:8, Colossians 3:23–24, 2 John 2–3, Revelation 22:12

CONSIDER

Jesus and His early followers often talked about receiving rich rewards in heaven. Of course, heaven itself is a reward of infinite value. Now, imagine the Lord giving you many specific rewards for your work here on earth. It's like receiving a Medal of Honor or gold medal, only so much better. Never apologize for seeking to earn rich rewards to enjoy for all eternity.

PONDER

* What's the greatest honor or reward you've received in this life?

* How does that compare with the rich rewards to be given in heaven?

* What's the greatest possible reward the Lord Jesus could give you?

More about We Can Look Forward to Rich Rewards: Matthew 6:4, Mark 9:41, Luke 6:23, Luke 6:35, 1 Corinthians 3:14, Hebrews 10:35

Topical Index